D1234333

What They Didn't Teach You in **German** Class

What They Didn't Teach You in **German** Class

Slang phrases for the café, club, bar, bedroom, ball game and more

Daniel Chaffey

Ulysses Press

Published by:
Ulysses Press
P.O. Box 3440
Berkeley, CA 94703
www.ulyssespress.com

ISBN: 978-1-61243-676-0
Library of Congress Control Number: 2016957794

Printed in the United States by Bang Printing
10 9 8 7 6 5 4 3 2 1

Managing editor: Claire Chun
Editors: Shayna Keyles, Alice Riegert
Proofreader: Renee Rutledge
Design and illustrations: what!design @ whatweb.com
Layout: Caety Klingman

Distributed by Publishers Group West

"Sag deinem Hauptmann:

Vor Ihro Kaiserliche Majestät hab ich, wie immer schuldigen Respekt.

Er aber, sag's ihm, er kann mich im Arsch lecken!"

—Götz von Berlichingen

Table of Contents

Using This Book

If you don't know the difference between *Scheiße* and *Schuhcreme*, this book might be a rude awakening for you. *What They Didn't Teach You in German* Class, written as a sort-of follow up to *Dirty German,* was written with the intermediate-level German speaker in mind, someone already familiar enough with the language to get by—but beginners and pros alike will find this book useful. Maybe you've got just enough *Deutsch* under your belt to read the menu at your local *Schnitzelhaus*, or maybe you're so hard-core you've memorized Goethe's *Faust* and can sing all your favorite *Rammstein* lyrics until your vocal cords burst into flames. Regardless of your current ability, this book will push you beyond what Frau Schmidt taught you in your Intro to German class and take your German to the next level so that you don't come off sounding like a total tourist.

Language is a living thing, and the German language is, in general, very regional. Whether you are in the North, South, East, or West, you'll likely find regional variants of words that you thought were familiar. As it would be exhaustive to catalog, categorize, and include these variations, I opted to include only those that you are most likely to encounter. With this in mind, remember that as you gain more confidence in speaking outside of the classroom, you may encounter terms that are not included in this book. This is a good thing. Think of this book as a set of tools that will open your language-learning eyes, ears, and mind. It will prepare you to transcend the barriers of stale, textbook dialogues and instead let you really engage in meaningful (and often meaningless) conversations with new friends.

The most important thing to know when you use the information and phrases in this book is context. Understanding the difference between formal and informal settings, and the communication requirements of each, is essential to getting by in German society. I can't emphasize this enough.

For the most part, this is a slang book, and often, a very dirty slang book. If you were to use the tips, phrases, and a large portion of the vocabulary within this book in a formal setting, it would be the social equivalent of crapping on someone's living room floor. Don't even think of using most of these phrases with people older than you, government officials, professors, cops, your friends' parents, or pretty much any strangers, unless you're ready to seriously offend someone.

That being said, feel free to throw out any of these gems when hanging out with your friends, your friends' friends, or anyone else you might know in a friendly setting; it's sure to increase your street cred. After all, this book focuses on language as it is used outside of the classroom, and it's filled with plenty of helpful phrases and info to help break down the language and cultural barrier. It may even get you a date! If you're afraid that you might offend someone, exercise caution and slowly slip into conversations with terms you find appropriate.

Grammar review

You'll be happy to see that lengthy grammar explanations and conjugation tables are missing from this book—after all, I don't want to bore the *Schnitzel* out of you with stuff you probably already know, or don't want to review. There are, however, a few important grammar-related points that need to be addressed. Of course, this is just a review of the stuff that you should still remember from your classes, even if they seem like ancient history.

All nouns in German have a gender that dictates their definite article (i.e., "the"). This gender plays a vitally important role in helping you understand what's going on in any given sentence. Gender affects adjective endings and changes in case—nominative for subjects, accusative for direct objects and objects of accusative prepositions, dative for indirect objects and objects of dative prepositions, as well as genitive for showing possession. (If you don't know what any of that means, you should probably look it up.) Since you must memorize the gender of a noun when you learn a new word, each noun's gender is labeled as follows:

(m) for masculine nouns, which take the article *der*

(f) for feminine nouns, which take the article *die*

(n) for neutral nouns, which take the article *das*

(pl) for plural nouns, which take the article *die*

Another issue that's difficult to remember, even for advanced students, is when to use the right endings for possessive pronouns (my, your, etc.). Since the gender and case of the noun dictates how the possessive pronoun ends, I give you the ending options in parentheses whenever I use a phrase in which a possessive pronoun needs an ending appropriate to the noun you use. For simplicity, all examples following a possessive pronoun will be given in the order of *das/die/der*. For example:

Slap my...!
Schlag mein- (-e, -en)...!

The above example covers your ass when telling someone to slap anything...regardless of whether it's a *das*, *die*, or *der* noun. These are the pronouns you'll need to keep in mind, and the endings that follow:

My	*mein/meine*
Your (informal singular)	*dein/deine*
Your (formal singular)	*Ihr/Ihre*
Her	*ihr/ihre*
His/its	*sein/seine*
Your (informal plural)	*euer/eure*
Your (formal plural)	*Ihr/Ihre*
Our	*unser/unsere*
Their	*ihr/ihre*

If the noun can be either male or female, the different endings will be included in parentheses, as seen in the examples below:

Bobbi is my boyfriend/girlfriend.
Bobbi ist mein(e) Freund(in).

I'm a friend of...
Ich bin ein(e) Freund(in) von...

Pronunciation

Because an extensive pronunciation guide would be way too long to fit within the introduction to this book and would never cover all of the many little nuances within the German language, here's a short intro addressing some of the more common pronunciation mistakes that even advanced students of German often make.

C sounds like the "ts" in "shits" before an i, ä, y, or e, and like the "k" in "kill" everywhere else.

G sounds like the "g" in "give" unless it follows a vowel at the end of a sentence, in which case you pronounce it with a soft "ch" sound, like in "ich."

J sounds like the "y" in "youth," never like the "j" in jackass, unless the word is of English origin, like "jazz." Words taken from French, like "journalist," have a French pronunciation of "j," like "zhuh."

Q sounds like the "q" in "question." Like in English, the "q" is always followed by a "u," but in German, it makes the Q sound like a "kv."

S sounds like the "z" in "zipper" before vowels and y, and like "sch" before t and p.

V almost always sounds like either the "f" in "father," and only in rare cases sounds like the "v" in "video."

W sounds like the "v" in "Vaseline."

X sounds like the "cks" in "sucks" (words beginning with X are rare).

Y sounds like the "oo" in "oops."

Z sounds like the "ts" in "cats."

Then there are the umlaut vowels.

ä sounds like the "e" in "ten," only longer.

ö sounds like the "i" in "stir."

ü sounds like the "ou" in "tour."

Some other tricky pronunciation issues:

au sounds like "ow" in "cow."

ae has the same pronunciation as "ä"; use this transcription for typing on non-German keyboards.

ah sounds like "a" in "car," but held a little longer.

äu sounds like "oy" in "boy."

ei sounds like "i" in "wine."

eu sounds like "oy" in "boy."

eh sounds like "a" in "day."

ie sounds like "ee" in "beer."

ieh also sounds like "ee" in "beer," same as "ie."

oe has the same pronunciation as "ö"; use this transcription for typing on non-German keyboards.

oh sounds like the "oa" in "boat."

ue has the same pronunciation as "ü"; use this transcription for typing on non-German keyboards.

uh sounds like "oo" in "too."

ch after a, o, or u is like the "ch" in Scottish "loch," spoken in the throat.

ch after i or e is like "h" in "huge."

ch at the beginning of a word is like "ch" in "chemicals" or like the h in "huge."

ck is like "ck" in "fucking."

ng is like "ng" in "ringing," never with a hard g like the "ng" in "finger."

ph is like "f" in "foot."

sch is like "sh" in "shit."

sp at the beginning of the word sounds like "shp" in "fish poop."

ss is like "ss" in "hiss," in contrast to "ß," which makes the preceding vowel shorter. "ss" is used in place of "ß" in URLs.

st at the beginning of a word is like "sht" in "ashtray."

Now drop your textbook, and get outta the classroom!

CHAPTER 1

Meet & Greet
Sich Kennenlernen

At first, Germans can come off as a little cold, standoffish, and intimidating. Don't take it personally. This distance is built into their language and their public lives, so they just need a little time to warm up to strangers. Think of them as New Yorkers without the brash attitudes. For the beginner, knowing how to be polite and when to use *Du* or *Sie* in the company of "Zee Germans" can be a little nerve-wracking. The tips in this chapter should help ease the tension and let you mix it up without sounding like a total tourist.

Hello
Hallo

Just like hello in English, *hallo* is a generic greeting that can be used anytime, with anyone, and just about everywhere, especially if you're speaking formally to someone, like a cop, whom you'd normally address with *Sie. Hallo* also makes it easier to say "hi" in different regions in Germany and in different German-speaking countries, where people have their own special ways of saying hello. But if you really want to break through the ice with your new German friends, try chopping it up with some more laid-back greetings.

Howdy!
Hallöchen!

Howdy-do!
Hallöchen mit Ö-chen!

Hey, hey, hey!
Halli-Hallo!

INTRODUCING YOURSELF
SICH VORSTELLEN

My name's Krissy.
Ich bin die Krissy.

I'm from Florida.
Ich komme aus Florida.

Yes, my suntan is real.
Ja, meine Bräune ist echt.

But no, I'm not a huge fan of nude beaches.
Aber ich bin kein grosser Fan von FKK Stränden.

I'm Kevin.
Ich bin der Kevin.

I'm from Alaska.
Ich komme aus Alaska.

I am a professional mountain climber.
Ich bin Bergsteiger von Beruf.

I'm totally ripped and hung like a stallion.
*Ich bin ein echter Muskelpietsch und auch **ein Drei-beiner**.*

There are also regional ways to say hello. Don't worry too much...these variations are understood throughout the German-speaking world, so just like if you walked into a bar in New York and said "Howdy," someone in Berlin would understand what you meant if you walked in saying *Servus*, or *Grüß Gott*. It just might come off as a little foreign.

Hi!
Hi! (everywhere)

Moin/Moinsen (northern and northwestern Germany)

Grüß Gott; Servus (southern Germany)

Servus (Austria)

Grüzi; Ciao (Switzerland)

Good morning/afternoon/ evening
Guten Morgen/Tag/Abend

Germans are stereotypically punctual and precise...some might say to a fault. Each time of day has its own special greeting and a slangy way of using it.

G'morning, everybody!
Morgenz!

Good morning, sleepy head!
Morgen Mäuschen!
Literally, "mornin', little mouse!" which sounds super cute.

G'day!
'Tach!

Hi, everyone!
Tag, zusammen!

Good afternoon!
Mahlzeit!
Mahlzeit is literally "meal time," but no one needs to be eating for you to say it.

Evenin'.
'Nabend.

Have a good one!
Schönen Abend noch!
Have a good *evening*, that is.

Nighty night!
Nachti Nacht!

How's it going?
Wie geht's dir?

"Wie geht's dir?" is like an old Nirvana T-shirt: It's comfortable, but a bit dated and worn out these days. Try one of these slangy versions instead. Just remember that Germans take questions like "what's up?" literally, so be prepared to hear more information than you need to know or be asked for more information than you might want to give.

What's up?
Wie geht's?

How's life?
Was Macht die Kunst?
Literally, "how are the arts?" Sure, it's from Lessing's 18th-century tragedy *Emilia Galotti*, but everyone uses it, not just brainiacs.

How's it hangin'?
Wie geht's, wie steht's?
Literally, "how's it standing?" Best used just with dudes.

What's going on?
Was ist los?
Literally, "what's loose?" or "what's wrong?" It loses its negative sense when used in this context.

Nothin' much!
Naja, es geht!
Literally, "it's going." A neutral response, this can be used to describe your mood, or to explain that nothing much is going on in your life.

I'm awesome!
Mir geht's glänzend!
Literally, "I'm doing brilliantly!" Use this when things are really going well.

I'm doing so-so.
Mir geht's so la-la.

Shitty, I just got canned.
***Beschissen**, mein Chef hat mich entlassen.*

Not so good, everything's all going downhill.
Nicht gerade gut, alles geht Bergab.

Awesome! I just got my dream job!
***Prima!** Ich habe endlich mein Traumjob!*

What's up?
Na?

In informal situations, "Hi, how's it going?" can be too long. Friends will often greet each other with just "*Na?*" It carries the same meaning, but saves you ten letters. You can also slap it on to the beginning of any statement to take things down a notch and make the whole statement seem more laid back.

Hey, bro, what's up?
Na, Alter?
Alter literally means "old man," but is regularly used to mean "bro" or "dude."

What's up, G?
Na, Alda?
Alter becomes *Alda* in punk, blue-collar, hip-hop, and other German slang cultures. It's kind of like how "gangster" becomes "gangsta" in the U.S.

Hey, sexy, what's up?
Na, Süße(r)?

What's up, jackass?
Na, Du Penner?
This term can be used seriously or jokingly, so watch your tone.

Hey ladies, what's up?
Na, Mädels?

Hey dudes, what's up?
Na, Jungs?

Well, lookie here...
Na, also....
This is almost always used as a smart reply, or expression of surprise.

Pleased to meet you!
Es freut mich dich kennen zu lernen!

The easiest way to get in with your new German peers is to find out about them and, especially, to let them know about you. Germans are really curious, and sometimes straight-up nosy. In any case, take their interest in you as a good sign. As an American foreigner, you'll be an object of interest and have an excellent chance to make some new friends. So just dive in and start chattin' it up.

Nice to meet you!
'Freut mich!

Sorry, I didn't catch your name.
Deinen Namen habe ich nicht mitgekriegt.

Who are you exactly?
Wer bist'n Du eigentlich?

My name's...
Ich bin...

How old did you say you were?
Wie alt bist Du denn?

How old do you think I look?
Wie alt sehe ich denn aus?

I'm a friend of...
Ich bin ein(e) Freund(in) von...

I'm new here in....
Ich bin neu hier in....

Got anything to drink?
Gibt's was zu trinken?

Is it OK if I smoke?
Geht es, wenn ich hier rauche?

Geht es? is an easy go-to phrase for checking to see if something is OK. It literally means, "does it go?"

Got a light?
Hast Du Feuer?

Thanks to the 2007 "Federal Law for the Protection of Non-smokers" (*das Bundesgesetz zum Nichtraucherschutz*), smoking in Germany was banned in essentially all enclosed public spaces; even bars and clubs. Smoking, however, is still generally accepted among most Germans, and plenty of café's, clubs, and bars have outdoor spaces for smokers.

LET'S SKIP THE FORMALITIES
LASS UNS DUZEN

The difference between using formal and informal German all depends on who you're addressing. Generally, you should address older people and people you deal with in professional settings (cops, bosses, coworkers, and anyone else you don't know) with *Sie*. When talking to your friends, animals, people younger than you, and family members (regardless of age), use *Du*. This distinction is so important to the Germans that there are actually verbs for using *Sie* (*siezen*) and *Du* (*duzen*). You can *duzen* fellow students (and coworkers, once you both agree on it), but you should *siezen* teachers and bosses. Although more and more Germans have become less strict about it, and many offer to use *Du* early on, it's like a rite of passage to be offered the ever-sacred *Du*. Here are some possible scenarios:

Mrs. Schmidt, we've been having sex for weeks now, don't you think we should **use "Du"**?
*Frau Schmidt, wir haben seit Wochen Sex, sollten wir uns jetzt nicht langsam mal **duzen**?*

Mr. Preuss, we've worked together for years and our families even go on vacation together. Shouldn't we **use "Du"**?
*Herr Preuss, wir arbeiten seit Jahren zusammen und fahren mit unseren Familien zusammen in den Urlaub. Sollten wir uns nicht **duzen**?*

OK, Mrs. Sander, but if I gotta screw you to get an A, can't we at least **use "Du"**?
*Na also, Frau Sander, wenn ich mich in Ihrer Klasse hochficken muss, dann sollten wir uns **duzen**?*

Do you work or are you still in college?
Arbeitest Du schon, oder studierst Du noch?

What else do you do for fun?
Was machst Du denn in deiner Freizeit?

Are all your friends this cool?
Sind alle deine Freunde so cool?

Are you from around here?
Kommst Du denn hier aus dieser Gegend?

Can you guys show us around the city?
Zeigt ihr uns ein bisschen von der Stadt?

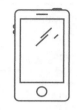

Can I give you my cell phone number?
Darf ich dir meine Handynummer geben?

Just text me!
Texte mir einfach!

Long time no see!
Lange nicht gesehen!

Catching up with old friends is just as important to Germans as it is for English speakers. Once the Germans have warmed up to you, they really let loose.

It's been a while!
Ist 'ne Weile her!

Where've ya been hiding?
Wo hast Du dich versteckt?

Everything cool?
Alles paletti?

I've been way too busy!
Ich habe viel um die Ohren gehabt!

Lookin' good, man!
Du siehst aber toll aus!

Man, you look like shit!
Du, siehst echt Scheiße aus!

Whatcha been up to?
Was gibt's Neues?

Same shit, different day!
Immer der gleiche Scheiß!

Man, I'm glad **you're doing so well!**
Alter, toll, dass es dir so gut geht!

You should **hang out more!**
Du solltest doch öfter abhängen!

Gimme a call sometime!
Ruf mich doch an!

I hope we **can hang out!**
Ich hoffe doch, dass wir abhängen können!

Please, thank you, you're welcome!
Bitte, danke, bitte!

Bitte can mean "please," "you're welcome," and even "excuse me," depending on how you use it. But friends aren't normally so polite around each other. They'll usually just use those hard-to-describe particles *doch* or *mal* to make demands of one another, the way friends in the U.S. do, as in: "Loan me a few bucks so I can buy a six-pack."

Pleeze!
Bötte!
This is something of a silly and whiny form of *bitte*.

Can you loan me five Euros, **pleeze**?
Leih mir doch fünf Euro, bötte?

Please please please!
Bitte bitte!

Pretty please?
Na Bittchen?
Literally, "little please."

Thanks a lot!
Vielen Dank!
Depending on the context and your tone, this can sound sarcastic.

Hey, grab me a beer!
Hol mir mal 'n Bier!

Chill out!
Chill doch!

Give it a shot!
Versuch's doch mal!

Do me a favor!
Tu mir doch einen Gefallen!

Thank you very much.
Danke sehr.

You're welcome.
Bitteschön.

Many thanks.
Tausend Dank.
Literally, "thousand thanks."

You're very welcome.
Bitte sehr.

It was my pleasure.
Gern geschehen.

No problem, anytime!
Kein Problem, gerne wieder.

I'm sorry!
Es tut mir Leid!

Es tut mir Leid ("It does sorrow to me") is the standard way to absolve yourself of guilt in German. Depending on the situation, there are varying degrees to which you can express your sorriness. Germans have a bunch of slangy ways to apologize for mistakes and take responsibility for their fuckups. Among friends, there are even ways you can be a jerk about it and still cleanse yourself of wrongdoing.

Sorry!
'Tut mir Leid!

Hey man, I'm so sorry!
Mensch, tut mir echt Leid!

I'm fucking sorry!
Tut mir fucking Leid!

Don't panic!
Keine Panik!

Excuse me!
Entschuldigung!

As in English, "excuse me" in German can be used to get someone's attention or to apologize for a party foul.

'Scuse me!
'Tschuldigung!

Excuse...
Verzeih mir...

> **my broke-ass German**
> *mein fieses Deutsch*

> **my B.O.**
> *mein Körpergeruch*

my bad breath
meinen Mundpups
Literally, "fart-mouth."

Oopsy!
Oopsala!

'Scuse me for burping!
Rülpsala!

'Scuse me for farting!
Furzsala!

Pardon me?/Come again?
Wie bitte?/Verzeihung?

It's no big deal!
Mach dir nichts daraus!

See you later!
Auf Wiedersehen!

Auf Wiedersehen literally means "until we see each other again," and implies that you actually desire to do so. As specific as Germans are about speech and, well, just about everything, this implies that you hope to literally see them again. Sometimes you really don't, though, so you might want to master some of these phrases to avoid giving the wrong impression.

Catch you later!
Bis die Tage!

See you soon!
Bis demnächst!

We'll see.
Mal sehen.
This is usually used in a negative sense, like "eh, maybe we won't."

See ya round!
Man sieht sich!

Smell ya later!
Bis Spinäter!
This is more of a frat-boyish term.

See ya!
Tschüß!

Bye!
Tschü!
As if *Tschüß!* wasn't short enough, sometimes folks drop off the ß to make things even shorter.

See ya later, alligator!
Tschüssikowski!
Kind of a cutesy term.

Bye-bye!
By-Di-By!

Safe drive home!
Kommt gut rein!
Literally, "get in there good," a smutty play on the harmless *Kommt gut Heim*—"get home safely." Best for when a couple is sneaking away to get it on, or you're wishing a buddy good luck on a date.

Talk to you later!
Wiederhören!
Usually reserved for phone calls.

Write ya later!
Wiedermailen!
A play on the Germanized *emailen*, this is usually reserved for emails.

CHAPTER 2

Friends & Family
Freunde & Familie

Just because your recent German friends have started to "*duzen*" you doesn't mean that you're BFFs. As a foreigner you're sort of a novelty, and most Germans will be interested in you and pretty outgoing because of it. But unlike your typical American, Germans see friendships as an investment. So it'll take a while before you guys will be tight like PB&J. There are varying degrees of friendship you'll likely progress through as you go from total stranger to *dicker Freund*.

Friends
Freunde

Stranger
Fremde (m/f)

> Some **stranger** walked up and smacked my ass!
> *Ein **Fremder** kam auf mich zu und packte mich am Arsch!*

My sister's **acquaintance** thinks you're really cool!
*Eine **Bekannte** von meiner Schwester findet dich total geil!*

A **girl in Stefan's class** is banging the professor.
*Eine **Mitstudentin von Stefan** vögelt den Prof.*

He's totally in love with his **coworker** Wolfgang.
*Er hat sich in seinen **Arbeitskollegen** Wolfgang verknallt.*

He's got no real friends, only **chat-buddies**.
*Der hat zwar keine echten Freunde, nur **Chatfreunde**.*

Pal/Buddy
Kumpel (m/f) (-in)

> Matthias is a **real pal**, he'll do just about anything!
> *Matthias ist ein echter **Kumpel**, der macht jeden Scheiß mit!*

Homie/Gangsta
Kollege (m/f) (-in)

A more slangy version of *Kumpel*, usually used among hip-hop kids and wanna-be gangstas.

> Watch it! Ertan's my **homie**. Got it?
> *Pass auf! Ertan ist 'n **Kollege**. Verstehst Du?*

Lothar is awesome. He's a real **no-bullshit kinda** guy.
*Lothar ist der Hammer. Ein **echt bodenständiger Kerl**.*

Best friends
dicke Freunde

Literally, "thick friends."

> Of course I loaned him my leather pants, we're **best friends**.
> *Klar, habe ich ihm meine Lederhose geliehen, wir sind doch **dicke Freunde**.*

We're stuck together like **white on rice**!
*Wir halten zusammen wie **Pech und Schwefel**!*

Literally, "like tar and sulfur."

Chitchat
Quatschen

As much as Germans pride themselves on their deep intellectual conversations, they still love to hang out, have a beer, and toss around some mindless bullshit. Save the Nietzsche for your thesis advisor or your boss and keep it light and breezy as you ease into the crowd.

To bullshit/shoot the shit/chitchat
Quatschen

> We just **shot the shit**.
> *Wir haben einfach **gequatscht**.*

Dude, where'd you get that sweet jacket?
Na, wo hast'e die geile Jacke her?

My friends back home would love you guys!
Meine Freunde zuhause fänden euch klasse!

So what's the deal with Oktoberfest anyway?
Na also wirklich, was ist mit dem Oktoberfest?

Do lots of German girls get **tramp-stamps**?
*Haben viele deutsche Mädels auch **Tussistempel**?*

Also commonly known as an *Arschgeweih* (ass antlers), these tattoos are the same the world over.

Wow, you look just like the singer from Tokio Hotel!
Wow, Du siehst aus wie der Typ von Tokio Hotel!

Are all Germans **sexy, smart, and funny**? Or just you?
*Sind alle Deutsche **sexy, lustig, und intelligent**? Oder nur Du?*

Hey, **you look really familiar**. You look just like my next boyfriend/girlfriend...
*Hey, **Du kommst mir so bekannt vor**. Du siehst aus wie mein(e) nächste(r) Freund(in)...*

Family
Die Familie

The modern German family can be just as normal or dysfunctional as its American cousin. Your new friends might have divorced parents, a trophy wife stepmom, two gay dads, or a creepy brother who lives in the basement playing video games all day. But no matter how cool their families seem to you, your friends are likely to complain about them. And just like in the States, regardless of how laid-back your friends might be with their own parental units, *you* still have to call them "Mr. and Mrs. So and So" and "*siezen*" them until offered otherwise.

Nice to meet you, **Mrs. Sander**.
*Es freut mich Sie kennen zu lernen, **Frau Sander**.*

A pleasure to make your acquaintance, **Mr. Sander**.
*Mich freut es Ihre Bekanntschaft zu machen, **Herr Sander**.*

You remind me a lot of **my mother**.
*Sie erinnern mich an **meine Mutter**.*

My mom's the nicest lady in the world.
Meine Mama ist die liebste Frau der Welt.

My **old lady** is a real bitch!
Meine Alte ist 'ne echte Ziege!

My father is a big softy at heart.
Mein Vater ist wie ein Kuscheltier.
Ein Kuscheltier is really a big stuffed animal.

My dad never calls on my birthday.
Mein Papa ruft mich nie zu meinem Geburtstag an.

My old man is a real alky!
Mein Alter ist voll der Säufer!

Personalities
Persönlichkeiten

The assortment of people you'll meet in Germany is as varied as the sausage selection at the local *Metzgerei* (butcher shop), and chances are that your new friends will have a slang term for each one.

Ain't you just the **sweetest thing**?
Bist Du nicht süß?

Jens is a real **likable guy**.
Der Jens ist ja wirklich ein sympatischer Typ.

Dorothea is a, **um, really nice girl**.
Dorothea ist ja ganz nett.

As in, "I can't think of anything good about this person so I'll call them 'really nice.'"

Martin is totally **antisocial**.
Martin ist echt der Asi.

Short for *Asozial*.

Ever since Otto barfed on my couch, he's **a total outcast**.
Seit Otto auf mein Sofa gekotzt hat, ist er echt das Schnitzelkind.

This term is pretty poetic in origin: This type of outsider (*Außenseiter*) is so much of an outcast, it's like he has to have meat tied around his neck to get a dog to play with him.

My boss is a real **dumb-ass**!
Mein Chef ist ein echter Kackspecht!

Literally, "shit woodpecker."

Hey **you idiot**, piss off!
Hey Du Spacko, verpiss dich!

Hey, watch out, **jerk-off**!
Eh, Du Wichser, pass auf!

GIRLFRIEND/BOYFRIEND OR JUST A FRIEND?
EIN(E) FREUND(IN), ODER EIN(E) FREUND(IN) VON DIR?

The German word for friend, *Freund*, shows no distinction between boyfriend/girlfriend and "just a friend." You need to take possession of your guy or girl by referring to them as "my" (*mein*), or distance yourself by using "of mine" (*von mir*). Otherwise, people might think you're banging your BFF. Try these examples on for size.

A friend
Ein(e) Freund(in) von mir

Detlev's my friend.
*Detlev ist ein **Freund von mir**.*

No, we're not screwing, **she's just a friend**!
*Nee, wir bumsen nicht, die ist nur 'ne **Freundin von mir**!*

Detlev is **my boyfriend**.
*Detlev ist **mein Freund**.*

Yeah, she was making out with **my girlfriend**!
*Ja, sie hat meine **Freundin** vollgeknutscht!*

Friend with benefits
der/die Fickfreund(in)

No, she's not really with him...he's just a **friend with benefits**.
*Die ist nicht wirklich mit ihm zusammen...er ist ihr **Fickfreund**.*

He's always got something shitty to say, the **smart-ass**.
*Der hat immer was schlaues zu erzählen, der **Klugscheißer**.*
Literally, a "clever shitter."

No job, no money, no chicks, what a **loser**!
*Kein Job, keine Knete, keine Perle, was für ein **Loser**!*

Since Klaus got fired, he's become a total **slacker**.
*Seitdem Klaus gefeuert wurde ist er voll der **Gammler**.*

Britta's new boyfriend is a total **stoner**!
*Brittas Neuer ist voll der **Kiffer**, eh!*

What, are you afraid, **mama's boy**?
*Watt denn **Müttersöhnchen**, haste' Schiss?*

You got no chance with her, bro, she's only into **muscleheads**.
*Mit ihr haste eh keine Chance, Alter, die steht nur auf **Muskelprotze**.*

....

Typically German
Typisch Deutsch

If you spend enough time people-watching in Germany, you'll start to notice how certain stock characters show up over and over again, just like how in every American high school you're guaranteed to find jocks, rednecks, preps, skater punks, stoners, and those super-shy kids who turn out to be total sex-fiends in college. Here's a list of those people that are sure to pop up during your time in Germany. Memorize it so you don't get laughed at for confusing a *Hopper* with a *Hipster*.

Studis

Studis, short for "students," love to party. The German university system is free of charge, which means most *Studis* live off their parents or the government. Since they don't really need to work, they are free to party their asses off. Don't get me wrong; the average German student is dedicated to their education, but the open enrollment policy means that *Studis* go to class whenever they feel like it with little repercussion. This leaves them free to rage at the many beginning- and end-of-semester parties (*Semesteranfangsparty/Semesterabschlußparty*) and hit up all the great bars and *Kneipen* (pubs), which all German university towns have in spades.

Do you know where all the **students** hang out?
*Weißt Du, wo die ganzen **Studis** herum hängen?*

Gruftis

These are Germany's answer to the goth kids who used to eat lunch in lonely, pale twosomes at your high school. Like their American counterparts, some in the *Grufti* spectrum are dark, sexy vampire types; but *Gruft* does mean "crypt," so the average *Grufti* looks like pale, warmed-over death. Their pasty complexions, dark eye makeup, black nail polish, knee-high boots, spiked leather trench coats, and long black hair (usually with some portion of it shaved to the skull) doesn't 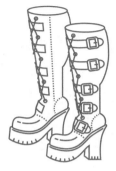 help either. Look past all that, though, and *Gruftis* will show you where the real nightlife is. Being nocturnal and all, they love to stay out all night, and they usually know where all the coolest clubs are. Try to tag along with a pack of them to a Dark-Ages Metal show where bands dressed up like Conan the Barbarian play speed metal with twelfth-century instruments and Latin lyrics...spooky! Every summer, the city of Leipzig hosts the *Wave-Gotik Treffen*, where twenty thousand goths meet up to get drunk, listen to bands, and avoid getting a tan.

Hopper

These blingin' kids represent German hip-hop. They're a mix of ethnic Germans, Turks, Greeks, Africans, and anyone else under the sun. What makes them interesting is how they've taken the best and worst of American hip-hop and tweaked it, Teuton-style. For instance, Germany has its own version of the East Coast/West Coast feud between Berlin and Hamburg. And although their fashion tends to follow American trends, you won't see many grillz or pimp cups. Berlin's heavyweight battle-rapper Sido used to wear a diamond-encrusted silver skull mask, though—that was pretty dope.

I can't take German **hip-hop kids** seriously.
*Ich kann die deutschen **Hopper** nicht ernst nehmen.*

Schickimickis

Schickimicki is a sarcastic play on *schick*, the German word for "chic." It's mostly used as an insult to describe something or someone that's supposed to be classy, but is usually just pretentious and obnoxious, like wine bars and reality show stars. Like "pretentious prick," the term is usually reserved for guys who think they're the shit; you know, the type that wears five-hundred-dollar sunglasses indoors, buys clothes that cost more than your car, and has a lifetime membership to the *Sonnenstudio* (tanning salon). Picture a European metrosexual with the asshole mindset of the captain of the football team.

There are way too many **pretentious pricks** here.
*Hier gibt's echt zu viele **Schickimickis**.*

Tussis

Tussis are usually found in packs of three or in the company of a *Schickimicki* guy. Like her male counterpart, the *Tussi* is generally a caricature of herself: super tan, particularly in the winter; gets her hair dyed either platinum blonde or jet black, with no variation; cell phone–dependent; and expensively, but not tastefully, dressed. Sure, she might study business or marketing, but her real goal is to become a trophy wife. She'll usually drop her boyfriend in a heartbeat, as soon as someone richer comes along. If Paris Hilton were German, she'd definitely be a *Tussi*.

Angeber

An *Angeber* (also known as a *Prahler* or a *Protz*) is just a run-of-the-mill show-off. They might try to impress you with their expensive stuff, or some new talent that they're dying to demonstrate, but don't confuse them with the *Schickimicki* crowd. They are really showing off to get your attention. More than anything, they want to fit in.

Oh man, Uwe's juggling knives again. What a **show-off**.
*Mann Mann Mann, Uwe jongliert schon wieder mit
Messern...der **Angeber**.*

Hipster

More of an adjective than a noun, German hipsters are just as
hard to nail down as their international counterparts. They're
marked by their insane desire to be different, or to be "true
individualists." And much like the hometown hipsters you may
know and love/loathe, they thrive on irony and the belief that
they don't belong to the rest of you. But they don't want to
belong, anyway. Don't get excited when you run across one, as
I'm sure they'll just be unimpressed.

All this **hipster shit** drives me nuts.
*Diese ganze **Hipsterkacke** bringt mich auf die Palme.*

Penner

This is a mildly derogatory term for Germany's homeless people,
or *Obdachlose*, kinda like calling them all bums. The term *Penner*
literally means one who sleeps, only I've never really seen a
Penner who was actually sleeping. They tend to hang out in
front of train stations and market squares. They are generally
harmless, unless they're drunk and start yelling at each other,
which can lead to a fight. Of course, feel free to label the jerk
that spilled his beer on you as a *Penner*, but just be prepared to
deal with the consequences.

I saw two **bums** yelling in front of the train station.
*Ich habe zwei brüllende **Penner** vor dem Bahnhof gesehen.*

Rocker

Rocker are a weird cross between greasers, party animals, and
the members of your local biker gang. Their typical uniform
consists of a leather vest with an old "Ace of Spades" T-shirt
underneath, a pair of lace-up-the-side leather pants, and biker
boots. They will drink you under the table and then beat you
over the head with it. They don't tend to mix with the general
public, but if you do manage to befriend one of these guys, be

sure to bring an extra liver because you're about to go on the bender of your sweet, young life.

Punker

More often than not, this is a squatter punk. Your hard-core German *Punker* has many of the same attributes of a *Penner*. They can be smelly, dirty, and usually hang out with a smelly, dirty, dog in front of a train station begging for change, but they sorta have an anarcho-punk agenda. Think Hollywood street kids or a squatter punk in a big city.

> German **punkers** look tougher than the punks back home.
> *Die deutschen **Punker** sehen echt härter aus als die Punker bei uns zuhause.*

Ökos

Your average German makes even hard-core American hippies look like seal-clubbing carnivores. In addition to introducing the world to Birkenstocks and communal nudism, the Germans, in general, are some of the world's best recyclers. The *Ökos*, however, take it to the extreme. Think of your worst "eco-freak" nightmare and then give them a degree in social pedagogy (kind of like a new-age, touchy-feely version of social work), and that's an *Öko*. *Ökos* are usually vegans, speak like they're talking to a five-year-old, drink Yogi Tea, wear purple socks, bathe infrequently, and seem like they're perpetually stoned even if they aren't. Try to avoid them...unless that's your thing, in which case you should be willing to shit in a bucket, chain yourself to a tree, or drink some homemade wine.

> **Eco-freaks** are a little too extreme for me.
> *Die **Ökos** sind mir etwas zu extrem.*

Aktenkacker

Literally a "file shitter," or an "office bee" (*Bürobiene*), if it's a woman. German office workers aren't your average overworked salarymen. They'll complain about only having six weeks of vacation a year, or how they had to work 32 hours last week and are totally worn out—they're definitely less hardcore than your over-the-top Japanese executive. Find them at an "After-work-party" (no kidding, that's what happy hour is called) in any downtown bar. They're pretty easy to spot: She's wearing a skirt and blazer with a brightly colored blouse. He's rocking a suit with a typically German blue dress shirt and some weird designer glasses that you've never seen before. Chat them up if you wish, but remember: At the end of the night, they're heading off together to screw and count their money.

> These **business-types** have way too much money.
> *Diese **Aktenkacker** haben echt zu viel Geld.*

Prolls

These guys are Germany's answer to rednecks, but they don't necessarily live in the sticks. Stereotypically, they're more prominent in the industrial north, but you can find them everywhere. You can spot them easily by their mullet/hair capes (*Nackenmähne*), track suits, creepy molestaches, and suped-up Opel Mantas—the German equivalent of the Trans Am. "*Proll*" comes from "Proletariat," and the name fits. They're Germany's blue-collar best, and for some reason they love parking lots. You can find them on the weekend hanging out at the local gas station, showing off their cars and blasting Böhse Onkelz tunes from their stereos. If you meet them in a beer tent at a local *Stadtfest*, watch out. They'll buy you round after round of *Lütt un' Lütt* (a beer and a shot) that'll get you smashed and have you singing *Volkslieder* until six in the morning.

> Does every **redneck** drive an Opel Manta?
> *Fährt jeder **Proll** einen Opel Manta?*

Omas und Opas

Grandmas and grandpas are everywhere in Germany, and German senior citizens are well looked after by the state and their families. *Omas* have a standard look: short and pleasantly plump, with their hair up in a bun, and they almost always wear a woolen coat and a fuzzy pastel

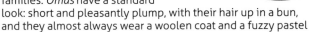

beret. They usually have a little dog with them, especially on the bus where they'll give you dirty looks for listening to your headphones too loudly. *Opas* usually wear some type of sweater vest and the standard Grandpa hat, the *Prinz Heinrich Mütze*, which is basically a Greek fishing cap made of wool. In the south, *Opas* might sport a Pinocchio-like *Alpenmütze* cap instead. Some *Omas* and *Opas* can be a bit crotchety since they lived through the Second World War, were POWs, and helped to rebuild their bombed-out country and all. So cut 'em some slack, and give up your seat on the bus with a smile.

German grandmas and grandpas are totally cute.
***Omas und Opas** sind voll süß.*

CHAPTER 3

Booze, Bars, & Clubs
Fusel, Kneipen, & Clubs

Despite their stereotype for being super punctual, hard-working clean-freaks, Germans love to party. The tips in this chapter will help you keep a cool head when getting your drink on, and distinguish between a *Vorglühen, Fest, Party, Feier*, and *Abtauparty*, even if you can't remember what happened when you were at each of them.

It's party time!
Jetzt geht's los!

When the average German leaves the office, it's all play and no business, and they try to keep it that way. *Feierabend*, which means "quitting time" in German, literally translates to "celebration evening," and it really is just that. When Germans get off work, the ties loosen, the formality disappears, and the beer starts flowing. It's the perfect time for you to pick up on how your German friends and coworkers really talk when they get down.

I wanna....
Ich will....

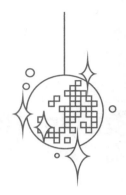

> **go downtown**
> *in die Stadt gehen*
>
> **go to the club**
> *in die Disko gehen*
>
> **get my groove on**
> *abhotten*
>
> find a **hottie**
> *'ne geile **Schnitte** finden*
>
> **meet up with friends**
> *ein paar Freunde treffen*
>
> hook up with a **chick**
> ***ein Püppchen** abschleppen*
>
> hook up with a **dude**
> ***einen Kerl** abschleppen*
>
> **get some action**
> *was Action*
>
> **haul ass**
> *abhauen*
>
> **get home soon**
> *bald nach hause*

Whadaya up to?
Was machste'?

No one, not even the serious and self-reliant Germans, likes to party alone. So don't be shy about inviting your new German friends out. Next time you wanna scope out the action for the weekend but don't know how to ask what your friends are up to, throw out a couple of these.

Whadaya up to?
Was machste'?

> **Nothin' much.**
> *Nix.*
> This Bavarian variant is essentially universal. Other options are *Nüscht*, used in northern Germany, and *Nischt*, used in Sachsen.

> **I'm bored out of my skull!**
> *Ich langweile mich zu Tode!*

Got any big plans for tonight?
Haste' heute Abend was Großartiges vor?

Whadaya wanna do?
Was willste' denn machen?

> **Dunno, any suggestions?**
> *Weiß nicht, haste' Vorschläge?*

> **Something cool.**
> *Was Cooles.*

> **Party hardy!**
> *Steil gehn!*

Go out and knock back a few...!
Ganz schön einen Bechern gehen...!
Literally, this means to go out for a mug (of something). Remember *der Becher* (the mug) from the unit in your textbook on dishes? This gives a whole new meaning to the word.

Are ya up for...?
Haste' Bock auf...?
Bock haben literally means "to have goat." The story goes that a male goat is very much driven by its desire, so much so that goats are used as the example for intense desire.

another beer
noch 'n Bierchen

somethin' to eat
was zu essen

barhopping
eine Kneipentour

smoking a fatty
dübeln

Bring it on!
Jetzt geht's los!

Nah, I'm not interested.
Nee, ich habe keinen Bock drauf.

Hey, let's....
Hey, lass uns....

go out for a smoke
eine smöken gehen

grab the **bong**
*die **Blubber** holen*
The name "*Blubber*" comes from the "blub blub" sound it makes
when you smoke it.

order **another round**
noch 'ne Runde bestellen

go to the **brothel**
*in den **Puff***

chill for a bit
mal chillen

make some **prank calls**
***Telefonterror** spielen*

Cause some trouble
stänkern

get nuts
auf die Katze treten
Literally, "step on the cat."

Gettin' down!
Die Sau rauslassen!

Lass die Sau raus translates as "let the pig loose," and means gettin' wild. But don't just scream it out like some drunken fratboy letting everyone know that he's getting his drink on. It's a German slang classic that is used loosely to describe the mood for some seriously wild partying. Let your friends know you're having a good time with some of these phrases.

Tonight....
Heute abend....

> **we're gonna go wild**
> *lassen wir die Sau raus*
>
> I wanna party **like never before**
> *will ich feiern* **wie noch nie**
>
> I'm gonna **get freaky** on the dance floor
> *werde ich auf der Tanzfläche richtig* **abspacken**
> If used outside the context of dancing, it means to act like a dumb-ass, so watch out.
>
> **I'm ready for anything**
> *bin für jeden Scheiß bereit*

I'm gonna **party all night**
*werde ich **durchfeiern***

I'm **having a blast**
*geht's mir **glänzend***

I'm gonna **raise the roof**
gebe** ich richtig **Gas
Literally, "step on the gas."

Chillin'
Chillen

Even hard-core partiers need a break every once in a while, and Germans are no different. Chillin' is so important to them that they even made up a new verb: *chillen*.

I just wanna **hang out** at home.
*Ich will zu hause **abhängen**.*

I'm gonna **chill** on the couch.
*Ich werde auf dem Sofa **chillen**.*

I'm gonna **veg out**.
*Ich werde nur **herumgammeln**.*
Literally, "to rot around."

I'm just gonna **grab a pizza**.
Ich hole mir einfach 'ne Pizza.

I feel like **watching a video**.
*Ich will 'n **Video gucken**.*

I'm just gonna **tug it** and fall asleep.
*Ich werde mir **einen runterholen** und einpennen.*

Party!
Es wird gefeiert!

Germans, like Eskimos and their infinite words for snow, seem to have a name for every type of party imaginable. Just slap "party" at the end of a noun or adjective and suddenly you have a whole new word to describe exactly how you're gonna get down. Here are just a few examples of the types of parties you're likely to encounter.

Vorglühen

Vorglühen is literally what you do to a diesel motor to warm it up. So in English, it translates to pre-gaming—you know, the partying before the actual party. You usually start drinking at someone's house before a night out, or you can even start on the way to the party. Drinking in public is allowed all over Germany, so buses, streetcars, trains, and corners are perfect spots for *vorglühen*.

> Christian **pre-gamed** so hard that he didn't even make it to the party.
> *Christian war schon beim **Vorglühen** total besoffen, dass er nicht zur Party gekommen ist.*

Semesteranfangsparty (f)

University students usually organize a "beginning-of-the-semester party," (or end-of-semester: *Semesterabschlußparty*) in one of the student housing complexes, which often come complete with a bar, dance floor, and enough outside space for a couple hundred students to get hammered in. Different departments talk smack about how great their parties will be. They're usually a bastion of drunken awesomeness, but if you choose the wrong one, you'll get stuck with a bunch of awkward people standing around trying to sound smart.

Man, the **business students** throw the best **end-of-semester parties**!
*Na, die **BWL-er schmeißen** wohl die besten Semesterabschlußpartys!*

Ballermannparty (f)

This is Germany's closest thing to spring break debauchery. Named after the popular Ballermann 6 beach bar on the Spanish island Mallorca, *Ballermannpartys* can be small private parties or huge events in a club. Most attendees are there to relive their drunken nights at the actual Ballermann bar from a previous vacation. Just like in Mallorca, there's lots of cheesy pop music, beach attire, and sleazy guys looking to get into any girl's pants. Think of a Teutonic version of your favorite Spring Break destination, and you'll get the picture.

Thorsten got totally trashed at that **Ballermann party** and was ready to fuck anything that moved.
*Thorsten war auf der **Ballermannparty** vollblau und wollte egal was durchficken.*

Grillparty/Gartenparty (f)

Basically the German version of a backyard cookout, only with way better food. During bikini weather, which in Germany usually means whenever the sun is shining, anyone with a backyard *Garten*, *Rooftop*, or *Hinterhof* (an enclosed courtyard of your apartment building) will invite friends over for a potluck-type bash with anything from *Sauerkraut* and *Schnitzel* to *Bratwürste* and beer.

Herms and Sabine are having a **barbecue** on Friday, but don't even think of bringing your crappy pasta salad.
*Freitag ist doch **Grillparty** bei Herms und Sabine, doch deinen eckligen Nudelsalat kannste vergessen.*

After-work-party (f)

This is basically happy hour. German clubs offer an *After-work-party* between 6 and 10 p.m. to attract young professionals.

Companies will even use them for "team-building," which is really just an excuse for a bunch of coworkers to get plastered together. But the Germans take this shit seriously. They have a phrase, "*Dienst ist Dienst und Schnaps ist Schnaps*," which means "duty is duty, and booze is booze." It's nice to see that they can keep their priorities straight.

> At **happy hour**, I got completely hammered and **made a pass at my boss**.
> *Auf der **After-work-party** war ich total besoffen und **hab' den Chef angebaggert**.*

Ü-30 (or Ü-35, Ü-40, Ü-50) Party (f)

These are similar to *After-work-partys*, in that they are marketing ploys made by some bars and clubs to attract specific clientele—only the Ü means *über*, and the number at the end means the party is strictly for crowds over 30, 35, 40, 50, or whatever age group is in the title of the party. Usually a mix of professionals and older partiers trying to stay away from clubs overcrowded with teenagers, the *Ü-30 Party* will usually play mostly 80's and 90's music, allowing the aging crowd to relive their youth without all the annoyance of a youth audience. Beware: If you fit the age and decide to attend, you'll never be able to say:

> I've never been to an **Over-30 Party**.
> *Ich war noch nie auf einer **Ü-30 Party**.*

Mottoparty (f)

These can be hosted anywhere, by anyone (privately, by an organization, or in a bar or club), and are based around a theme, or motto. Some examples are the All-white-party (don't worry, the guests are just supposed to show up wearing all white); *Komm-wie-Du-bist-Party* (the come-as-you-are party), where the guests have to arrive wearing only what they had on when they opened the invitation, even if they were nude; or the *Böse Überraschung Party* (the terrible surprise party), where each guest receives an invitation to a different themed party, with the end result that they show up dressed for the wrong party, and are in for a terrible surprise. Talk about *Schadenfreude*.

Abiball (m)

Although this is the German version of prom night mixed with high school graduation night, *Abiball* still deserves mentioning, even if you are closer to attending your first *Ü-30 Party*. Who knows, maybe you're teaching in Germany and need to help organize it. Pupils at the local *Gymnasium* (think high school on steroids) have one last time to be together as a graduating class before receiving their *Abitur* (think high school diploma on steroids), and this is the *Abiball*. They can be based on a theme and have different programs and events associated with them, but the thing to remember is that the average pupil is old enough to drink, and it is OK to do so...even with teachers, on school property. It's crazy.

> The **Abiball** is next week and I have nothing to wear!
> Der **Abiball** ist nächste Woche und ich habe nichts zum Anziehen!

Abtauparty (f)

This "thawing out party" isn't really a party at all, but the feeble attempt at recovering from your hangover with a little "hair of the dog that bit you."

> Damn, I feel like shit. I think I need a little "**hair of the dog**."
> Mannomann ist mir schlecht. Ich brauch' 'ne **Abtauparty**.

Where Germans hang out
Wo die Deutschen feiern

Lokal (n)

This catch-all term is used for any local spot. It can be a bar, a pub, or a restaurant, but it usually refers to the neighborhood place you and your friends will always go to, and suggests this spot sorta means, "Hey, let's go out and grab a bite or hang out."

> **Hey, wanna go out and grab a bite/drink?**
> *Hey, wollen wir ins Lokal?*

Kneipe (f)

Germany's answer to the pub. They're cozy and offer food and some entertainment in a laid-back, unpretentious environment. This is where most Germans go to have a beer, a bite to eat, and maybe listen to some live music and enjoy the atmosphere. It's the perfect place to end a hard day's work or begin a hard night's partying.

> Wouldn't you rather just go to the **pub** instead of some shitty disco?
> *Wolltest Du nicht lieber in die **Kneipe** gehen, statt in die scheiß Disko?*

Disko (f)

These generic dance clubs can sometimes be cool, but are usually overrun by techno-loving teens and tools trying to hook-up with Kardashian wannabes. They may or may not be host to the next *After-work* or *Ü-30* party.

> Man, these fucking **discos** drive me insane.
> *Na also, diese scheiß **Diskos** gehen mir echt auf den Sack.*

Club (m)

A *Club* is much less annoying than a *Disko,* since this is where you'll see cool bands in a smaller setting. And getting to the bar is a whole lot less crowded, too.

> The SO36 is the coolest **club** in Berlin.
> *SO36 ist der geilste **Club** in Berlin.*
> This particular club in Berlin was originally a 19th-century beer garden, later a movie theater, and ultimately one of Berlin's most provocative locations for music and art. Named after the old SO36 postal code for the district of Kreuzberg (known for its diversity,

subcultures, and everything "non-German"), the club became a haven for artists, musicians, and other dilettantes in the 1970s and 1980s. The club was the center of a scene that rivaled New York City, and the famous CBGB. Luckily, SO36 is still open and carries on the same countercultural spirit.

Bar (f)

Plain old bars—which are strictly for booze and never offer food—are a bit of a rarity in Germany. Since Germans love to eat and dance when getting hammered, they usually only end up in one of these at the end of an evening out. More often than not, it's a bar in a *Disko* or attached to a café. The Capri Bar in Bremen is a good one to check out if you get the chance—it's decked out like a cave inside.

> Nah, the bar's **stupid**. Let's go somewhere else instead.
> *Nee, die Bar ist **doof**. Lass uns mal woanders hin.*

Lounge (f)

An ultra-trendy bar for people who'd rather get drunk sipping overpriced cocktails while sitting in expensive pieces of furniture than standing at a bar with all the riff-raff. They can be cool, but are usually pretentious.

> This lounge is totally boring, **let's bail**.
> *Also, diese Lounge ist absolut tote Hose, **lass uns leine ziehen**.*
>
> *Tote Hose* literally means "dead trousers," which I guess are really boring. *Leine ziehen* means to pull the reigns, and get a move on.

Gaststätte (e)/Gasthof (m)

There's no really good English translation for these establishments that are closer to a restaurant than a pub, but have the laid-back atmosphere of a pub. They're kind of like old-school gastropubs. Though *Gaststätten* aren't particularly cool, go here when food is more important than booze and you don't want to lose your shirt on the bill.

The *Gaststätten* in this town are nothing special, but the food is really good.

*Die **Gaststätten** dieser Stadt sind nichts besonderes, aber das Essen ist total lecker.*

Café (n)

Somewhere between a bar/restaurant and a *Kneipe,* your local *Café* is usually a good spot to stop in any time of day for a coffee or a beer, and even a bite. Drop in if you feel like having a beer during the day, but don't really want to go to a pub. Café Eisen in Bremen is in the Ostertorviertel, or the Ostertor District, which is full of museums, galleries, and movie theaters.

Hey, let's stop at the *Café* after we hit the museum!

Hey, lass uns nach dem Museum ins Café gehen!

Bahnhof (m)

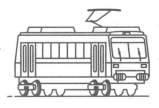

There's something very liberating about getting sloshed in public with your friends while waiting for the last train home. Since you can drink in public, the train station is one of the best places for *Vorglühen* (pre-gaming) or even an *Abtauparty*.

Timm and I missed the last train, so we just got tanked at the **train station** and waited it out.

*Timm und ich haben den letzten Zug verpasst und kippten deshalb am **Bahnhof** ein paar Bierchen weg.*

Kiez (m)/Viertel (n)

The *Kiez* or *Viertel* is a general term for a cool district or neighborhood, like the French Quarter in New Orleans or the Village in New York, where there are tons of clubs, pubs, and restaurants. In Hamburg, the *Kiez* is St. Pauli, home to the infamous *Reeperbahn*, the red-light district known as The Sinful Mile, which is full of strip clubs, sex shops, and brothels.

Hey, wanna roll down to the *Kiez* and **see what's going on**?
*Wollen wir mal auf'n **Kiez** und **die Lage abchecken**?*

Rotlichtviertel (n)

Prostitution is alive and well in Germany. You'll find one of these red-light districts in pretty much any big city. In Hamburg, it is a blocked-off street in St. Pauli, conveniently next to a police station. In Düsseldorf, there's a building near the main train station, or *Hauptbahnhof,* where the ladies of the evening sit in windows that display their room numbers so lonely businessmen can make their choices before they even get off the train. Sorry, ladies; these are men-only zones.

Only **creeps** hang out in the **red-light district**.
*Nur **Fieslinge** hängen im **Rotlichtviertel** rum.*

Nutten gucken

Nutten gucken is a verb for groups of bored, drunk dudes who love to stop by the red-light district and check out the ladies of the evening. It's like window-shopping for love without catching any STDs, but also a sure sign that your evening is quickly coming to an end.

Dude, I'm bored outta my skull, let's go **check out some hookers**!
*Na Alda, mir ist strunzlangweilig, lass uns **Nutten gucken**!*

Go-Go Bar (f)

This isn't a nudie bar; it's just a place with a bunch of scantily clad women dancing and serving really expensive drinks. The beer might cost you 20 dollars, but for you ladies and gents who are into that sort of thing, the *Go-Go Bar* offers all the creepiness of a *Stripclub*, without the nudity.

I'm sick of all those **cock-teases** at the Go-Go Bar.
*Von den **Flittchen** in der Go-Go Bar habe ich's echt satt.*

Stripclub (m)/Striplokal (n)

Some things need no translation. This is a straight-up nudie bar. These can usually be found near a *Bahnhof* or in the *Rotlichtviertel*. You'd think that legal brothels would make these kinds of things obsolete, but businessmen and bachelor parties can't seem to get enough of 'em. Most don't have a men-only policy like the red-light district, so even ladies can go and be pervy in public.

> I blew my whole paycheck at the nudie bar. **My wife's gonna kill me!**
> *Das ganze Geld habe ich im Stripclub weggeschmissen.* **Meine Alte bringt mich um!**

Stadtfest/Schützenfest/Fest (n) or Kirmes (f)

This is kinda like a county fair, but with better food, fewer ex-con carny folk, and more drunks. Each year, every city will have at least one of these things, usually around a holiday. They're like mini Oktoberfests with all of the beer but none of the lame-ass tourists. If you get a chance, check out a *Schützenfest*. It's fuckin' nuts! It's got all the same rides, beer, and food as a *Stadtfest* or *Kirmes*, but it's also part of a huge party held after a massive shooting competition. That's right: drunk Germans with big-ass guns.

> Let's go to the **fair**. I wanna get **sloshed** and ride the roller coaster.
> *Lass uns mal zum* **Stadtfest**. *Ich will* **saufen** *und Achterbahn fahren.*

Booze
Fusel

At first glance, Germans might seem like a bunch of drunks, because booze is everywhere: bars, restaurants, corner shops, train stations, food kiosks. You can even buy beer at the Golden Arches. Beer is definitely the Fatherland's most popular social lubricant, but Germans also drink their fare share of wine and, of course, *Schnaps*. Whatever you're drinking, there are a few phrases you'll need to know to help ease you into inebriation.

Wanna drink?
Willste' was trinken?

Whadaya got to drink?
Was gibt's zu trinken?

Shouldn't we make a toast?
Sollten wir nicht anstoßen?
Look everyone in the eye when toasting, otherwise you'll be cursed with bad sex.

Cheers!
Prost!

Less talkin', more drinkin'!
Nicht lang schnacken, Kopp im Nacken!
Used in Northern Germany, this phrase literally means, "cut the chatter, tip your head into your neck."

Here's to...!
Auf...!

> **getting plastered**
> *breit werden*
>
> **unemployment**
> *die Arbeitslosigkeit*
>
> **alcohol poisoning**
> *Alkoholvergiftung*
>
> all my old girlfriends (boyfriends)! May they **burn in Hell**!
> *meine Ex-freundinnen (Ex-freunde)! Mögen sie in **der Hölle schmoren**!*

To your health!
Zum Wohl!
Normally used just with wine or *Schnaps*.

Down the hatch!
Prösterchen!

....

Beer
Bier

Beer is to Germans what wine is to the Italians, cheese is to the French, and chocolate is to the Belgians. Here's what you need to know to talk beer.

What's **on tap**?
*Was gibt's **vom Fass**?*

Do you only have **beer in bottles**?
*Habt ihr nur **Flaschenbier**?*

Most *Kneipen*, *Bars*, and *Gaststätten* have regional beers and maybe a larger national one on tap, while clubs usually stick to bottles.

Hey guys, what's the **local beer**?
*Hey Jungs, was ist denn **das Regionalbier**?*

Hey, how's about we go out tonight and **crack a few cold ones**.
*Mensch, lass uns heute Abend **ein kühles Blondes zischen** gehen.*

So, what's the deal with this **beer purity law**?
*Also, was ist mit dem **Reinheitsgebot**?*

This 19th-century national law limited beer's ingredients to water, barley, and hops to ensure purity. You'll still see "brewed according to the national purity law" on plenty of beers today.

Hey, wanna bust out the **beer-bong**?
*Na, wollen wir **trichtern**?*

Literally, "to do the funnel."

What the fuck, you've only got shit-beer?
*Was soll das denn, nur **Aldi-beer**?*
Aldi is a discount grocery store that usually has cheap discount beer.

Hey, I'm gonna grab some **brews**, ya want one?
*Na, ich geh mal **Bierchen** holen, soll ich dir was mitbringen?*

Drink! Drink! Drink!
Heu! Heu! Heu!
Someone yells "*Zicke Zicke Zicke Zacke!*" then everyone shouts back "*Heu! Heu! Heu!*" and then everyone drinks! drinks! drinks!

German beer
Deutsches Bier

Märzen-Oktoberfestbier (n)
This deep amber lager is the official beer of Oktoberfest and is brewed in the springtime only by breweries within Munich's city limits (*März* means "March"). By the time these beers make it to the Oktoberfest, they've been aged in caves and have an alcohol content of like six percent. *Prost!*

Hefeweizen (m)
Unfiltered wheat beer which is hugely popular in the south, but enjoyed everywhere. If you're getting trashed in a *Biergarten* in Bavaria, it's probably on this.

Kristallweizen (m)
The filtered version of a Hefeweizen.

Kölsch (n)
This pale, light-bodied, beer with a high alcohol content is served in small glasses. In order to be called a true Kölsch, it has to be brewed in and around Köln (Cologne). If you are in Köln for *Karneval* (essentially, the German Mardi Gras), watch out; you'll likely follow your newfound friends from one local brewery to

the next and drink too much of this, thinking that nothing so potent can come in such a small glass. It will kick your ass.

Schwarzbier (n)

Similar to a *Rauchbier*, or smoked beer, it's a really dark lager beer with a full, smoky, almost chocolatey flavor. It's almost like Guinness or any other stout, but since it isn't a stout, it's less heavy. Köstritzer is the best.

Bockbier (n)

It's an amber, heavy-bodied, bittersweet lager named after a male goat. Drink enough and it feels like one rammed you in the head.

Pilsner (also Pils) (n)

Really, the most popular beer. It's a light-bodied, hoppy lager (the bitterness depends on the brewery) that everyone drinks year round. Since it's available throughout the country all the time, try out some different regional versions for a real beer tour of Germany. Jever from the north is really hoppy and bitter. Radeberger and Wernesgrüner are from the old East Germany; both are now widely available and amazing.

Berliner Weisse (mit Schuß)

This pale, very sour wheat beer is brewed in Berlin. It's so sour you'll usually drink it mixed with a shot (*Schuß*) of either Raspberry (red) or Waldmeister (green) syrup. Waldmeister tastes like liquid cotton candy, so take the appropriate precautions.

Radler (m)/Alsterwasser (n)

Both refer to a Shandy, or the perfect balance of lemonade and beer. *Radler* (or bike-rider) got its name somewhere in the 19th century, when cycling gained popularity. In Hamburg and parts of Northern Germany, it's an *Alsterwasser*, or just an *Alster*, named after the refreshing waters of the Alster, a tributary of the Elbe River. In Bavaria, it's also known as a *Russ* (or Russian), and in areas near the French border it is refered to as *Panasch*. No matter what you call it, it refreshes the thirsty sports enthusiasts with its lower alcohol content.

Alkoholfreies

Of course, now knowing what constitutes a beer according to the *Reinheitsgebot* (beer purity law), this alcohol-free version is still techinically beer. Sure, you'll likely have friends who will call you out for drinking one, but there are some great non-alcoholic beers from German breweries. If you do, or don't want to get drunk, pay attention to the label, and drink accordingly.

Malzbier

If the thought of a dark malt beverage whets your whistle, then perhaps a *Malzbier* is for you. Although it looks like and is brewed like beer, the fermentation process is cut off before alcohol can be produced. It's syrupy-sweet and is the closest thing that Germans have to root beer. However, most Germans don't like root beer, and most non-Germans don't like *Malzbier*. Since it's considered a "healthy" alternative to soda, it's also referred to as *Kinderbier*, or Kid's Beer, and our son loves it.

Hard alcohol
Schnaps

In just about any German *Kneipe*, you'll see a couple of *Underberg Gürtel* hanging from behind the bar. These things look like Pancho Villa's bullet belt, but instead of holding bullets, they hold 20 little bottles of *Underberg*, an herb-based aperitif. At 44 percent alcohol, it packs a punch. The belts are mostly just for decoration, but when you get two dumb-asses drunk enough to challenge each other to *Wettsaufen* (competition drinking), the belts come down and the first person to get alcohol poisoning wins.

You wanna have a go at the **Underberg Belts**?
*Sollten wir mal **den Gürtel** holen?*

A shot
Schuß (m)

A double
Doppel
Combine it with your favorite booze: *Doppelvodka, Doppelwhisky*, etc.

On the rocks
auf Eis
Even just "on the rocks" in a really cool German accent will work.

Straight up
Pur

The well brand
Hausmarke (f)/des Hauses
Always used in conjunction with your alcohol of choice: *Whisky des Hauses, Vodka des Hauses*, etc.

Don't confuse *Schnaps* with the peppermint, peach, or cinnamon swill most high-schoolers get drunk on. It is really just a catch-all term for hard alcohol, and here are some classic fall-on-your-face favorites.

Obstbrand /Obstler(m)
Schnaps made from fruit wine, and it's as powerful as nitroglycerin.

Korn (m)
60-proof grain alcohol that tastes like paint thinner unless mixed with something else.

Doppelkorn (m)
80-proof *Korn*, which is even worse tasting than the 60-proof variety.

DRINKING SONGS
SAUFLIEDER

Germans love to sing drinking songs when they're getting hammered in beer tents and at fairs. There are lots of traditional classics, but they'll usually latch onto whatever crappy pop song fits with getting shitfaced. Sometimes the song is actually good and becomes a classic in its own right, like this song "Sauflied" by the German punk band Die Ärzte.

Ich und meine Kumpels, wir sind ein duftes Team
Wir sind regelrechte Alkoholvernichtungsmaschin'
Wir saufen bis zum Umfall'n, alle machen mit
Und wenn wir dann besoffen sind, dann sing' wir unser Lied

Komm, wir grölen noch ein bißchen, denn ich bin schon wieder voll
Komm, wir singen übers Saufen, über Bier und Alkohol.

Me and all of my buddies, we're a bad-ass horde
We're a bunch of alcohol-burning machines
We drink until we fall down and everyone's on board
And whenever we get fucked up, this is what we sing

Come on let's get loud in here, cuz my belly's getting full
Come and sing about drinkin', 'bout beer and alcohol.

Sing this one if you're getting plastered on *Bommerlunder*.

Eisgekühlter Bommerlunder,
Bommerlunder eisgekühlt.
Eisgekühlter Bommerlunder,
Bommerlunder eisgekühlt.

Und dazu:
Ein belegtes Brot mit Schinken—Schinken!
Ein belegtes Brot mit Ei—Ei!
Das sind zwei belegte Brote,
Eins mit Schinken uns eins mit Ei.

Ice cold *Bommerlunder*,
Bommerlunder, ice cold.
Ice cold *Bommerlunder*,
Bommerlunder, ice cold.

And then:
A little sandwich with ham—Ham!
A little sandwich with eggs—Eggs!
You've a couple of little sandwiches,
One with ham and one with eggs.

Magenbitter (m)

"Stomach bitters" is an aperitif, but most people knock it back in shots. Jägermeister and Underberg are the most well-known brands. Too many of these, and you're on your way to a coma.

Bommerlunder (m)

A German "Aquavit" type of licorice-flavored booze that's usually served in chilled shots and has even inspired a drinking song from German punk band Die Toten Hosen. Be sure to sing both verses at increasing speed until you can't sing any faster or you puke your drunk-ass guts out, whichever comes first.

Gettin' blitzed
Breit werden

Wanna **toss back a couple cold ones**?
*Wollen wir **ein paar Bierchen wegkippen**?*

I'm....
Ich....

> **buzzed**
> *bin gut drauf*

> **gettin' tipsy**
> *werde etwas beschwipst*

drunk
bin ganz schön betrunken

wasted
besoffen

smashed
bin total angeschickert

getting really fucking hammered
werde vollbreit
Literally, "getting wide."

drunk off my ass
bin total lattenstramm
Literally, "laid out like planks of wood."

I'm **drunk as a skunk.**
*Ich bin so **breit wie ein Biberschwanz**.*
Literally, "as wide as a beaver's tail."

I'm kinda **dizzy.**
*Mir wird's **schwindelig**.*

I'm gonna be sick.
Mir wird's schlecht.

I think **I'm gonna ralph.**
*Ich muss mit **Jörg** telefonieren.*
Literally, "to call Jörg." Like Ralph, Jörg is a name that sounds like puking.

Dude, tell me what I did last night , **I totally blacked out.**
*Mensch, ich **habe voll den Filmriss**, was habe ich gestern getan?*
This is like when the film in your head breaks, and suddenly, you're missing a scene.

I've got the worst **hangover.**
*Ich habe voll den **Affen/Kater**.*
Literally, "to have an ape/tomcat."

He's a total **drinking machine.**
*Er ist ein echter **Kampftrinker**.*
Literally, "combat drinker."

He can barely stand up!
Der Typ da nimmt schon Bodenprobe!
Literally, "that guy is taking samples of the floor"

Man, you can **barely walk straight.**
*Alter, Du bist ja voll **kursiv unterwegs**.*
Literally, "walking cursively."

She's so drunk, she's **speaking gibberish.**
*Die ist so dicht, dass sie die **Muttersprache verloren hat**.*
Literally, "losing your mother tongue."

You're a total **alcoholic.**
*Du bist voll **der Alkomat**.*

Germans are the coolest **drunks.**
*Die Deutschen sind die coolsten **Säufer**.*

VOMITOLOGY
KOTZOLOGIE

I gotta....
Ich muss....

vomit	*mich erbrechen*
puke	*kotzen*
throw up	*mich übergeben*
barf	*göbeln*
blow chunks	*den Döner abwürfeln*
hurl	*kübeln*
spew	*reihern*
yak	*abbröckeln*

Weed
Gras

German law regarding weed is weird and is in constant flux. Recent adjustments to medical marijuana laws in Germany do mean that those with a prescription will have easier access, but recreational use is still illegal. It's sorta decriminalized, meaning they won't pop you just for being high. But you can't buy, sell, grow, hold, or distribute weed. Nevertheless, even little cities have head/grow shops (*Headshops/Growshops*). They sell everything from papers (*Blättchen*) to bongs (*Bongs*) to pipes (*Pfeifen*) and hookahs (*Wasserpfeifen*), all of which are sold under the guise of regular tobacco use.

Germany is smack in the middle of Europe and the north of the country borders Holland, so there's a steady supply of high-quality weed right next door, which by default spills over the border. Most cops in big cities overlook pot and focus on hard drugs. But Bavarian cops can be hard-asses about it. They often target backpackers who wanna get lit before hitting Oktoberfest. German stoner-speak uses tons of English terms, but your buds (pun intended) will definitely have their own code words for all things cheeba.

Dude, I wanna **get baked**.
*Hay, ich will nach **Maryland fahren**.*
Literally, "drive to Mary (Jane) land."

Hey, wanna **smoke some hash**?
*Na, wollen wir **einen harzen**?*
Harzen means "to exude resin."

I don't have a **piece**.
*Kein **Fuckel**.*

It's time to roll that shit!
Na los, aufwickeln!

Sorry, bra, I barely got enough for **a pinner**.
*Sorry Alter, das hier reicht nicht mal für **einen Sticky**.*

Can you really get some **Amsterdam bud**?
*Kannste' wirklich was **Dutch** besorgen?*

Roller's rights!
Wer baut, der haut!
This literally means, "you built it, you hit it!"

Holy shit, man, you never hit the **gravity bong** before? It's the bomb!
*Bhoa Digga, niemals **Eimer geraucht**? Ist doch voll geil!*
Literally, "smoke the bucket." Some may know this as doing "bucket rips," but either way, it is the Big Bertha of bongs.

I've never seen a **spliff** that big before, it's like a baby arm!
*So 'ne **Tüte** habe ich noch nie gesehen, die ist doch riesig!*
Tüte is short for the giant cone-shaped *Schultüte* filled with candy and presents that German kids get on their first day of school.

I'm jonesing for **a joint** right now.
*Ich hab' voll Bock auf 'ne **Sportzigarette**.*

Will you show me how to roll a blunt?
Zeigst Du mir wie man eine rollt?

Let's **hotbox** the bathroom.
*Lass uns auf dem Klo **hotboxen**.*

I'm so **high** right now.
*Ich bin total **bekifft**.*

FIELDS OF GREEN
BLÜHENDE LANDSCHAFTEN

Weed
Weed

Hash
Haschisch

Bud
Pott

Chronic
Chronic

Reefer
Shit

Mary Jane
Maryland

Green
was Grünes
Literally, "some green."

Ganja
Ganja

Grass
Gras

Check him out, man, he's totally **faded**.
*Hey guck mal, der ist voll **benebelt**.*
Literally, "fogged up."

Wanna get somethin' to eat? I totally got **the munchies**.
*Willste was essen? Ich hab' voll **den Fresskick**.*

Bro, you're such a **pothead**.
*Na Alda, Du bist ja voll der **Kiffer**.*

Hard drugs
Harte Drogen

I don't need to say that cocaine is a helluva drug; just ask Rick James. Oh wait. You can't. That shit killed him. Even if some German cops might turn a blind eye to someone smoking a joint, they still take hard drugs pretty seriously and will throw your ass in prison for a long haul if they catch you with anything. Although Germany doesn't really have the same drug problems as, say, the United States, you'll still spot a junkie or a meth-head, now and again, hanging out in unsavory parts of town, or at the train and subway stations in bigger cities like Hamburg, Berlin, or Frankfurt. The following terms will help you figure out if you are suddenly in the middle of a situation you'd rather not be in.

Hey, you got anything stronger?
Hey, hast Du was härteres?

Know where I can **score** some...
Wo kriege ich was...

No thanks...**ain't my thing**.
Nee...ist nichts für mich.

> **coke**
> *Koks (m)*

> **crack**
> *Crack (m)*

> **heroin**
> *Heroin (n)*

shrooms
Fliegepilze (pl)
Literally, "flying mushrooms."

ecstasy
Extasy (n)

pills
Pillen (pl)

meth
Meth

acid
LSD

Get away from me, you **junkie**.
Hey Du Junkie, hau ab.

That guy ain't nothing but a **cokehead.**
Der Typ da ist voll der Koksnase.

Whoa, that dude's **covered in track marks!**
Bhoa, der da ist voll der Kanülen-Pete!

CHAPTER 4

Sexy Body, Ugly Body
Sexy Körper, Hässlicher Körper

Sexy Germans
Sexy Deutsche

Nowadays, sexiness is pretty much universal, and the average German's take on hotness is no different than the average American's, meaning everyone has different tastes and opinions on what they find attractive. Should you find yourself among friends and needing to describe your soulmate, or even just the date you had last night, try throwing a few of these terms around.

She's/He's....
Sie/Er ist....

> **kinda tall**
> *etwas größer*
>
> **charming**
> *charmant*
>
> **cute**
> *hübsch*
> Mostly used to describe girls.

pretty
schön
Used to describe girls.

handsome
herrlich
Used to describe guys.

gorgeous
hinreißend

hot
scharf

ripped
muskelbepackt

tan
gebräunt

cool
cool

stylish
modisch

sporty
sportlich

slim
schlank

well-groomed
gepflegt

He/She is a real hottie.
Er/Sie ist eine ganz heiße Nummer.

She's/He's got....
Sie/Er hat....

a cute smile
ein schönes Lächeln

beautiful eyes
wunderschöne Augen

a great face
ein tolles Gesicht

a toned figure
eine sportliche Figur

a great attitude
eine nette Ausstrahlung

a firm ass
'nen knackigen Arsch

I'm lookin' for a girl who's got some **junk in the trunk.**
*Ich brauch' 'n Mädel mit 'ner **Ködelkiste**.*

I guess you can't really get **a six-pack** just by drinking 'em, can you?
*Mann kriegt warscheinlich kein **Waschbrett** vom Saufen, oder?*

Dude, you're built like Arnold (Schwarzenegger)!
Mensch, Du bist echt der Arnie!

Ugly Germans
Hässliche Deutsche

Spend enough time in Germany and you'll quickly see that not everyone looks like they stepped off of the runway at a Berlin fashion show—there are plenty of folks who look more like they got run over on the *Autobahn*. In Germany, it's not polite to stare and make jokes about the hideously ugly, so wait until Frankenstein's monster has left before you ridicule them to your friends.

She's/He's....
Sie/Er ....

> **kinda short**
> *ist etwas kleiner*
>
> **awkward**
> *ist ungeschickt*
>
> **boring**
> *ist langweilig*
>
> **unattractive**
> *ist reizlos*
>
> **ugly**
> *ist hässlich*
>
> **nasty**
> *ist grässlich*
>
> **not too stylish**
> *ist unmodisch*
>
> **not very sporty**
> *ist unsportlich*
>
> **chubby**
> *ist pummelig*
>
> **husky**
> *ist kräftig*
>
> **fat**
> *ist fett*
>
> **unkempt**
> *ist ungepflegt*

unpopular with the guys/girls
ist unbeliebt bei Jungs/Mädchen

cross-eyed
shielt

fugly
ist ein echtes Gesichtsdresden
Dresden was bombed flat in the Second World War, so this is pretty fuckin' ugly.

butt-white
ist voll das Kellerkind
Literally, "cellar-kid," like a video game junkie.

a tub o' lard
ist ein Fettbatzen

a bean pole
ist ein langer Lulatsch
This refers to the radio tower in Berlin.

an Amazon (woman)
ist eine Amazone

tiny
ist Zwerg-mäßig
Literally, "gnomish."

kinda wimpy
ist ein Weichei
Literally, a "soft egg."

effeminate
ist ein Sitzpinkler/ein Warmduscher
Literally meaning "one who pees sitting down," or "one who takes warm showers." These terms are reserved for men (especially those who are sensitive about their masculinity).

ditzy
ist eine blöde Kuh/Ziege
Literally, "a dumb cow/goat." This term is just used for girls.

a hunchback
ist etwas buckelig

She's/He's got....
Sie/Er hat....

a crooked smile
ein kaputtes Lächeln

dumbo ears
Segelohren
Literally, "ears like sails."

bug-eyes
Glubschaugen

love-handles
Griffe am Arsch
Literally, "ass-handles."

plumber's crack
echt das Bauarbeiter-Dekolleté
Literally, "construction-worker cleavage."

stinky feet
Käsemauken
This refers to particularly stinky cheese.

Can you see my **fat rolls**?
*Kannst Du meine **Speckrollen** sehen?*
Literally, *"bacon rolls."*

I'm starting to get **a beer belly.**
*Ich kriege langsam 'nen **Waschtrommelbauch**.*
Literally, "a belly like a washtub."

Hair
Haar

OK, I know what you're thinking...German women don't shave. In reality, the days of the hairy-legged *Fräulein* are long gone. Nowadays, there's nothing a German woman or man wouldn't shave. Nonetheless, a lot of Krauts do still have some weird-ass body hair and some hilarious ways to describe it. Here are a few to look out for.

Achseldackel (m)
Extremely hairy armpits. Literally, "an armpit Dachshund."

Alfstrumpfhose (f)
Remember that incredibly bad TV show *ALF*? He was a hairy little alien that for some reason the Germans were, and still are, crazy about. So if your legs are insanely hairy, you've got "Alf socks."

O-li-ba (m)
Short for *Ober-Lippen-Bart*, or "upper lip beard." Moustaches suck, so make fun of dudes who have 'em, especially hipsters who think moustaches are funny and ironic.

Vo-ku-hi-la (m)
Means short in the front (*vorne kurz*), long in the back (*hinten lang*). You may call it a mullet, hair cape, or Kentucky waterfall, and think it looks like hillbilly shit, but certain Germans love this style, which is extremely popular among *Prolls* and *Rockers*.

Geburtsrahmen (m)
Literally, a "birth frame." Ever notice how a full beard resembles the "beard" babies get when coming out of their mama?

Gesichtsfotze (f)
If you think about it, "face-pussy" is a pretty perfect description of a goatee.

Bauklammer (m)
A moustache that looks like the giant construction staple for which it's named. Think of a "BGM" or Hulk Hogan's walrus 'stache.

Silberrücken (m)
This description of insane back hair is taken from "Silverback" gorillas.

Brustpullover (m)
Think of a sweater made out of chest hair.

Farting
Furzen

Most Germans will be discreet and excuse themselves to go drop an air biscuit. When you consider that the stereotypical German diet consists of beer, cheese, *Sauerkraut*, and sausage, you'd be amazed that the whole country doesn't go up in flames every time someone lights a cigarette. So, thank God, the Germans have banned smoking in most enclosed public spaces.

A fart
Furz (m)

To fart
furzen

To pass gas
blähen

To toot
pupsen

Hey, hold your breath, I'm gonna **crack one off**.
*Eh, Luft anhalten, ich muss **einen abdrücken**.*
Literally, "pull the trigger."

You just bust ass?
Haste' gefurzt?

Did you just shit your pants?
Haste' geschissen?
This is best used for a really wet one.

Hey, man, it wasn't me, must have been a **barking spider**.
*Hey ich war's nicht, wir haben **Brüllmücken** im Haus.*
Literally, "roaring mosquitos."

Dude, why are you always **lettin' 'em rip**?
*Eh, warum musst Du ständig **einen ziehen lassen**?*

Hey **butt-trumpet**, quit farting!
*Hey Du **Arschpfeife**, hör auf zu pupsen!*

I hear you can singe your ass-hair off by **lighting your farts**.
*Hab' mal gehört, dass man bei einem **Afterburner** die Arschhaare absengt.*

I think that one's gonna leave some **skid marks**.
*Die Nummer wird aber **Bremsstreifen** hinterlassen.*

....

Shitting
Scheißen

I don't know about you, but for me, takin' a dump in a public restroom can be pretty traumatic. In Germany, though, public pooping can be a thing of beauty. Most public restrooms have attendants who are supposed to keep things squeaky clean, unlike those diarrhea-blasted holes they call toilets in some other European cities. Most larger cities will have "pay as you go" automatic self-cleaning restroom kiosks located around town, sort of like ATMs for your BM. Going even further, a select handful of German train stations are home to the McClean, the Neuschwannstein of German shithouses. These graffiti-free, designer poop palaces have automatically opening frosted-glass entrances, no-touch flushes and faucets, air fresheners, classical music, and are always clean and sparkly. They're so inviting that never again will you be afraid to drop a deuce in public.

I gotta....
Ich muss mal....

poop
kacken

shit
scheißen

take a dump
einen abseilen
Literally, "to lower one down on a rope."

take a crap
böllern

A turd
Kacke (f)

A pile of shit
Scheißhaufen (m)

The runs
Dünnschiss (f)
Literally, "thin shit."

Explosive diarrhea
Flitzekacke (f)
Literally, "shooting or whirring crap."

I need to go **poo-poo**.
Ich muss A-A machen.
Pronounced Ah-Ah, this is a kinda cutesy term, since A-A is baby poop.

I gotta go **pinch a loaf**.
Ich muss ja einen abkneifen.

It's time to drop the kids off at the pool.
Ich muss Bob in die Bahn werfen.
Literally, "to throw Bob onto the train."

This morning I had a major hangover and some **serious beer shits** too!
Heute Morgen war ich voll Verkatert und hatte auch Gumobischi dazu!
Drunk Germans love nothing more than inventing new words by stringing together a bunch of other words and then abbreviating them. *Gumobischi* is one such abbreviation, short for *Guten Morgen Bierschiss*—the "good morning beer shit" you experience when mud starts raining out of your butt the morning after a night of heavy drinking.

That was a real **ring stinger**!
Das war voll der Rosettenbrand!

I'm pretty **backed up**.
Ich bin ja voll verstopft.

Aaaaaah! That felt like I was **shitting boulders**.
Mann Mann Mann! Das war voll der Brikettschiss.

Ulrich has to shave his ass, otherwise he gets **dingle berries**.
Der Ulrich rasiert sich den After, sonst kriegt er Klabusterbeeren.

That's way **too much fuckin' information**.
Echt zu viele fucking Infos.

Hey, hand me a roll of **shit tickets**?
*Hol mir die **Böllerpappe**?*

Holy fuck, did **someone die in here**?
*Scheiße eh, **liegt hier 'n toter Esel inner Ecke**, oder was?*
Literally, "is there a dead donkey in the corner?"

Pissing
Pissen

You might see this elsewhere, even at home, but lots of German urinals have a little fly painted on the inside of the bowl for guys to use as a target. It's close enough to the drain and set at just the right angle so if you hit the fly, you don't get any dreaded backsplash. It's kinda hard to concentrate when you're completely drunk, but it still helps prevent you from pissing on your Adidas. How's that for German engineering?

Pee
Pipi (n)

Piss
Pisse (f)

Urine
Urin (m)

I gots to go.
Ich muss mal.

I gotta pee again already.
Ich muss schon wieder Pipi machen.

I'm gonna go **take a leak**.
*Ich geh' mal **austreten**.*
Literally, "to step out of formation."

That dude just **whizzed** in the pool!
*Der Typ hat eben gerade ins Becken **gepinkelt**!*

Uh-oh, yellow alert!
Oh-oh, Alarmstufe Gelb!

Do you get the **piss shivers** too?
*Zitterst Du auch beim **Pullern**?*

How are you supposed to take a leak when you wake up with a **major piss-boner**?
*Wie kannste' schiffen wenn Du mit 'ner **ChroMoPiLa** aufwachst?*
ChroMoPiLa is short for *Chronische Morgenpisslatte*. The need to piss is what distinguishes this from the regular "morning wood" or *AlMoPraLa— All morgentliche Prachtlatte*.

I think I'm gonna take a **piss** here in the bushes.
*Ich geh' mal hinter'm Gebusche **schiffen**.*

Hey, how about **pissing for distance**?
*Na, wie wär's mit **Wettpissen**?*

Do German girls always **go pee in groups** like American girls?
*Sind alle deutsche Mädchen **Rudelpisser**, wie die amerikanischen Mädels?*

....

Assorted bodily fluids and oddities
Körperflüssigkeiten und Anderes

Popel, or "booger," is an extremely useful word. It's used as a compound noun for eye-boogers and earwax, as well as its own verb. Some Germans are totally cool with picking their nose (or almost any other orifice) in public, so don't be surprised if, mid-conversation, someone starts pickin' some nose gold, rolls it up, and drops it on the floor without even pausing to say "excuse me." Here are a few phrases to express your disgust with your friends' filthy behavior.

Dude, quit **picking your nose**!
*Mensch, hör auf zu **popeln**!*

Check out that kid, he's **totally nose drilling**.
*Schau mal, der Typ **bohrt voll in die Nase**.*

Wipe up your **snot**!
*Wisch dir den **Schnotten** ab!*

You got a **Kleenex?**
*Haste mal 'n **Tempos**?*

Tempos is the major German brand of tissue, and most Germans refer to the handkerchief from your textbook (*Taschentuch*) simply as a Tempos.

I caught him **eating his boogers**.
*Ihn habe ich beim **Popelfressen** erwischt.*

Fuck, man, my nose ring is all infected and **oozing puss**.
*Scheiße ähh, mein Nasenring ist voll infiziert und **vereitert**.*

Can you **pop this zit** for me?
*Kannst Du mir mal diesen **Pickel platzen**?*

I get insane **nosebleeds** when I'm drunk.
*Ich kriege voll die **Nasenblutung**, wenn ich besoffen bin.*

Why do you always smell your **earwax**?
*Wiseo musst Du denn deinen **Ohrenpopel** riechen?*

I slept so long my eyelids got glued shut with **eye-boogers**.
*Ich hab so lange geschlafen, dass meine Augenlider mit **Augenpopel** zugeklebt waren.*

I've never seen **dick cheese** before.
Nillenkäse habe ich noch nie live gesehen.

I've got this nasty **whitehead** on my butt cheek.
*Ich habe voll den **Packel** auf meiner Arschbacke.*

I was a total **pizza face** in high school.
*In der Schule, war ich voll die **Gesichtspizza**.*

I can't go into the pool, I just got **my period**.
*Ich kann nicht ins Schwimmbad gehen, ich habe meine **Tage**.*

Where can I buy some **tampons**?
*Wo kann ich **Tampons** kaufen?*

Who uses **pads** anyway?
*Wer benutzt noch **Damenbinden**?*

....

General sickness
Übelkeit

When asked, most Germans love to talk about how sick
they are, and many will go see a doctor at the slightest sign
of a cold. Don't jump to conclusions and think that they're
a bunch of whiny hypochondriacs; it's likely because their
healthcare system kicks the American healthcare system in
the taco. Anyway, I slammed my thumb in a car door and got
patched up for like five bucks, so I'm not complaining.

I'm feeling kinda **yucky**.
*Mir ist **schlecht**.*

Man, you **look pretty shitty**.
*Mensch, Du **siehst aber scheiße aus**.*

I'm not doin' so hot today.
Heute geht's mir nicht so gut.

You're looking a **little pale**.
*Du siehst aber **blass** aus.*

I just puked my guts out.
Ich ließ mir das Essen durch den Schädel gehen.
Literally, "to let your food out through your skull."

I've got **leprosy** and my nipples are falling off.
*Ich habe **Lepra** und mir fallen die Brustwarzen ab.*

Call an **ambulance**, damn it!
*Ruf doch den **Krankenwagen**!*
A German ambulance is literally "the sick wagon."

I need some **drugs**!
*Ich brauche **Drogen**!*

I'm stayin' home from work today. I got a **really nasty cold**.
*Ich geh heute nicht zur Arbeit. Ich hab' **Schnodderseuche**.*

I've got....
Ich habe....

> **a headache**
> *Gehirnmauke (pl)*
> Literally, "a withering, aging brain."

> **a migraine**
> *Migräne (f)*

> **a stomachache**
> *Magenschmerzen (pl)*

> **a sore throat**
> *Halskratzen (n)*

> **the flu**
> *eine Grippe (f)*

crabs
Sackratten (pl)

herpes
Herpes (m)

a serious hangover
voll den Schädelfraß (m)
Like moths eating away at your skull.

a case of the clap
voll die Rüsselseuche

a visit from Aunt Flo
Besuch von Tante Ruth
In Germany, it's your Aunt Ruth who comes a callin' once a month, not your Aunt Flo.

CHAPTER 5

Nice & Naughty
Gut & Böse

....

Fucking
Ficken

Germans are known throughout the world as über-geeks because of their fascination with order and accuracy. While that may be true, Germans, like everyone else, still love to bang. That doesn't mean that their slang for the deed isn't subject to order and accuracy, however. For instance, some Germans will actually describe sex as "sticking your pissing utensils together." Now, that's German precision, baby!

Your place, my place, or any place?
Zu Dir, zur Mir, oder einfach hier?

Are you as horny as I am?
Bist Du so geil wie ich?

I'm totally hot for you, let's...
Ich bin super heiß auf dich, wollen wir mal...

Let's go to my place and...
Lass uns zu mir gehen und...

Do you wanna talk all night, or do you wanna...?
Willst Du mich volllabern, oder willst Du...?

> **hump**
> *poppen*
> This is kind of a silly term.

> **fuck**
> *ficken*

> **fuck like bunnies**
> *wie Kanninchen rammeln*

> **do it**
> *es tun*

> **have a quickie**
> *einen Quickie haben*

> **hit it/bone/nail it**
> *bocken/hämmern/nageln*

> **lay some pipe**
> *das Rohr verlegen*

> **screw**
> *vögeln*

> **bump uglies**
> *das Pissgeschirr zusammen stecken*
> Literally, "to stick our pissing utensils together."

Wanna have period sex?
Willst Du ins rote Meer stechen?
This literally means "stab into the red sea." Doesn't that sound more adventurous?

You can fuck me in the ass!
Mir kannst Du die Muffe vergolden!

Genitalia, etc.
Schämikalien

Goethe is known as Germany's greatest poet and philosopher, but he was also an anatomist. He discovered the intermaxillary bone, which in German historical importance ranks just behind the invention of the printing press, the Protestant Reformation, and the mass production of Oktoberfest mugs. What does Goethe's "bone discovery" mean to you? Well, it links your investigation of human anatomy to a great philosopher, and makes you seem like less of a perv for wanting to say "Lick my *Knackmumu*."

Lick my...!
Leck mein- (-e, -en)...!

Stroke my...!
Streichel mein- (-e, -en)...!

Suck my...!
Saug/Lutsch mein- (-e, -en)...!

Slap my...!
Schlag mein- (-e, -en)...!

I love (your)...
Ich liebe (dein, -e, -en)...

I can never get enough...!
Von...kriege ich nie genug!

Let me take a picture of your...!
Lass mich ein Foto von dein- (-em,-er, -en)...knipsen!

Can I shave your...?
Darf ich dein- (-e, -en)...rasieren?

pussy
Muschi (f)/
Muschi originally meant pussycat and referred to the animal. Nowadays, it just means pussy.

cunt
Fotze (f)

hairy beaver
Fellfrosch (m)
Literally, "furry frog."

shaved pussy
Schoßglatze (f)

pussy hawk
Irokese (m)
Literally, the "Iroquois Mohawk."

clit
Perle (f)

pussy lips
Schamlappen (f)

tight pussy
Knackmumu (f)

cameltoe
Cameltoe (n)

pussy juice
Mösensaft (m)

cock
Schwanz (m)

johnson
Lümmel (m)

THE SAUSAGE TRAY
DIE WURSTPLATTE

When it's crunch time, or a task at hand is really important, Germans like to say *Es geht um die Wurst*, or "it's all for the sausage," because traditionally sausages were prized delicacies. Fortunately, little has changed. Like the selection of sausages available in a German deli, the variety of names for a man's best friend is just as diverse.

huge cock
Riesenschwanz (m)

hung like a horse
Pferdeschwanz (m)
Literally, "ponytail."

tiny dick
Pimmelchen (n)

limp dick
Schlapschwanz (m)
Schlapnudel (f)

big dick
Fleischpeitsche (pf)
Literally, "flesh whip."

shriveled dick
KaWaMiPi
Short for *Kalt Wasser Mini Pimmel*—"cold water dick."

dick
Puller (m)

prick
Hammer (m)

wiener
Wurst (f)

pecker
Pimmel (m)

pork sword
Fleischlanze (f)

trouser snake
Aal (m)

boner
Latte (f)
Literally, "plank."

head
Helm (m)
Literally, "helmet."

rim of the head
Eichelkranz (m)
Literally, "crown of the acorn."

foreskin
Kragen (m)/Bananenschale (f)
Literally, "collar" and "banana peel."

nuts
Nüsse (pl)

nads
Klöten (pl)

balls
Eier (pl)

ball sack
Sack (m)

pubes
Schamhaar (n)
Literally, "the hair of shame."

Tits and ass
Möpse und Kiste

Let me touch your...
Lass mich dein- (-e, -en)...anfassen.

Let me suck on your...
Lass mich an dein- (-e, -en)...lutschen.

Let me spank your...
Lass mich dein- (-e, -en)...knallen.

Let me fuck your...
Lass mich dein- (-e, -en)...ficken.

Nibble on my....
Knabberst Du an meine....

Wanna massage my...?
Massierst Du meine...?

> **tits**
> *Titten (f)*
>
> **hooters**
> *Hupen (f)*
> Literally, "honkers."
>
> **jugs**
> *Dinger (f)*
>
> **puppies**
> *Möpse (f)*
>
> **nipples**
> *Schnuller (f)*
> Literally, "pacifier."
>
> **nips**
> *Nippel (f)*

BOOBS
DIE MOLKEREI

All breasts are beautiful, from A to DDD.

mosquito bites
Mückenstiche (pl)

breastless
Flachland (n)

flat-chested
Bügelbrett (n)

barely-breasted
BMW (Brett mit Warzen)
Literally, "a board with nipples."

medium-breasted
pralle Titten (pl)
Plump, but not too big.

well-endowed
viel Holz vor der Hütte haben
Literally, "a lot of wood in front of the cabin."

Big tits
dicke Hupen

ginormous tits
Dickmanns (pl)
This name refers to a marshmallow candy that resembles large breasts.

beautiful tits
Porschetitten (pl)
The sportscar of tits.

fake tits
Kunsttitten (pl)

erect nipples
Igelnasen (f)
Literally, "hedgehog noses."

nipple ring
Nippelknochen (m)

ass
Arsch (m)

butt
Po (m)

rear
Hintern (m)

booty
Kiste (f)

ass crack
Po-Rille (f)

asshole
Rosette (f)

hairy asshole
Afterbart (m)

the taint
Damm (m)

Sex acts
Geschlechtsverkehr

Your textbooks have likely taught you the clinical term for sex: *Geschlechtsverkehr*, or "Gender Traffic." Don't be fooled. As silly as this description sounds, the average German is far more creative both linguistically, as well as sexually, when it comes to describing and performing the "dirty deed." Of course, you'll likely get by with the English terms, but go native and try some of these out.

Wanna try...?
Willst Du mal...ausprobieren?

I like...
Ich stehe auf...

I'm tired of...
Ich habe genug von...

...is boring.
...ist langweilig.

...gets me hot.
...macht mich heiß.

...turns me on.
...macht mich an.

> **kissing**
> *Knutschen*
>
> **cuddling**
> *Kuscheln*
>
> **dry humping**
> *Petting*
>
> **finger banging**
> *Fingerficken*
>
> **cunnilingus**
> *Muschilecken/Fotzenlecken*
>
> **fellatio**
> *Blasen*

playing the skin flute
(spielen) Flötensolo (f)
Literally, "a flute solo."

swallowing
Schlücken

facials
ins Gesicht abspritzen
Literally, "spraying into the face."

pearl necklaces
Schneebart (m)
Literally, "snow beard."

titty-fucking
Tittenficken

missionary style
Bambi-sex

doggy style
Hündchenstellung (f)
Also just referred to as "doggy-style."

woman on top
Frau-oben

Wanna give me head?
Willst Du mir einen blasen?

Wanna eat me out?
Willst Du meine Muschi lecken?

Wanna take me from behind?
Nimmst Du mich von Hinten?

Sexcessories
Fickzeuge

Because the only thing that should come between you and your partner is a condom...or a strap-on dildo, and some lube, and maybe some hot wax.

Do you have (a)...?
Hast Du mal (ein, eine, einen)...?

Let's try using (a)...
Lass uns mal (ein, eine, einen)...benutzten.

I never screw without (a)....
Ohne (ein, eine, einen)...bumse ich nicht.

> **rubber**
> *Gummi (m)*

> **condom**
> *Condom (m)*

> **sex toy**
> *Sex-spielzeug (n)*
> Also, the English "sex-toy" is used.

> **lube**
> *Gleitmittel (n)*

> **dildo/double dildo**
> *Dildo (m)/Doppeldildo (m)*

> **ass beads**
> *Lustkugeln (pl)*

> **butt plug**
> *Po-stöpsel (m)*

strap-on
Umschnaller (m)

vibrator
Vibrator (m)

handcuffs
Handschellen (pl)

whip
Peitsche (f)

mask
Maske (f)

rubber suit
Gummianzug (m)

cigarette
Kippe (f)

enema
Einlauf (m)

hot wax
heißes Wachs

chains
Ketten (pl)

Belt
Gürtel (m)

Kink
Bizarres

Sure, the Japanese invented Bukkake and the Dutch are notorious for Zoophilia, and thanks to *South Park*, I'm sure you've heard all about German *Scheiße*-porn! German society is all about structure, order, and discipline. So it's not surprising that in their private lives, some Germans are prone to weird sex and crazy fetishes. Berlin, Cologne, Hamburg, Vienna, and plenty of other cities have huge networks of fetish clubs, swinger bars, and brothels. Berlin's long-standing swinger club *Bar Möchtegern* is always free for the ladies, and they give out free drinks on the weekends. Go there to watch some guy get spanked with a Bible while you find someone to pee on. Here are a few terms to help you either find or avoid the darker side.

Be gentle with me!
Sei sanft mit mir!

Be rough with me!
Sei hart mit mir!

Be strict with me!
Sei streng mit mir!

Fuck my brains out!
Fick mich durch!

Whip me!
Peitsch mich aus!

Fuck me!
Fick mich!

I'm into....
Ich steh auf....

Let's try....
Lass uns mal...austesten?

> **rough sex**
> *harten Sex*

threesome
Dreier

group sex
Rudelbumsen

bisexual sex
Bi-sex

bondage
Fesselspiele (pl)

S&M
Sado-Maso Spiele (pl)

wax play
Wachsspiele (pl)

The suffix -*spiele* can be added to your favorite perversion to create a whole new lexicon of kink.

Boarding School Sex
Internatssex (m)

Germans are almost as excited about sex scenarios surrounding discipline and punishment in boarding schools as they are about beer and soccer.

anal sex
Po-Sex (m)

red wings
Rotbart (m)

female ejaculation
Mösensprudel (m)

scat
Naturkaviar (n)
Literally, "nature's caviar."

fisting
Faustficken

golden shower
jemanden anpinkeln (to give)/*...sich anpinkeln lassen* (to receive)

piss drinking
Natursekt trinken
Literally, "to drink natural Champagne."

COME AGAIN?
WIE BITTE?

Mmmm, I want to drink up your...!
Ich will dein-(-e, -en)...abtrinken!

sperm
Sperma (n)

cum
Ficksahne (f)
Literally, "fuck sauce."

jizz
Pilzsauce (f)
Literally, "mushroom sauce."

twat sauce
Fotzensaft (m)

cream
Schlagsahne (f)

tongue bath
Zungenbad (n)

vomit sex
Römern
Literally, "to do the Roman." *Römern* is a versatile verb meaning anything from scat and watersports, to erotic vomiting and just plain screwing. Basically, anything that is sexually deviant can be considered *Römern*.

Getting to know you (sexually)
Sich kennenlernen (durch Sex)

Germans aren't all blonde-haired, blue-eyed, *Lederhosen*-
and *Dirndl*-wearing caricatures from some Disney fairy
tale. Deep down inside many of them are sluts, pervs, and
fiends, just like you. So ditch the boring phrases from those
lame getting-to-know-you games you played in class (no
one gives a shit whether your favorite color is blue, or that
you *really* like pizza) and ask the questions that truly matter.

Are you (a)...?
Bist Du ein (-e, -en)...?

> **straight/hetero**
> *straight/hetero*

> **gay**
> *Schwule (m)/schwul (adj.)*
> Not pejorative, per se, but be careful.

> **fag**
> *Schwuchtel (m)*
> Certainly used as a derogatory term, and included here to help
> you identify it, if you hear it.

> **queen**
> *Tunte (f)*

> **drag queen**
> *Transe (f)*

> **lesbian**
> *Lesbe (f)/lesbisch (adj.)*

butch lesbian
Kampflesbe (f)
Literally, "combat lesbian." Often a pejorative, but also a reclaimed term used by the LGBT community.

lipstick lesbian
"LiStiLe" (f)/Lippenstift Lesbe

bisexual guy
Bi-Mann (m)/Bi-Jung
Just plain *Bi* is used for both men and women.

bisexual girl
Bi-Frau (f)/Bi-Mädel

Queer
Queer
For all LGBT uses.

Transgender
Transgender
Can be shortened to *Trans*.

Transexual
Transsexuelle

Transvestite/Cross-dresser
Transvestit (m)

Sexual deviancy
Sexuelle Abweichung

slut
Schlampe (f) (male or female)

bitch
Zicke (f)

cheap fuck
Hobby-nutte (f)

lousy lay
Schlefi (m) (male or female)

whore
Hure (f)/Nutte (f)

town whore
Dorf-Matratze (f)
Literally, "village mattress."

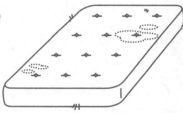

girl who sleeps her way to the top
Abi-nutte (f)
Abitur is the equivalent of high school graduation; *Abi* is the abbreviation.

virgin
Jungfrau (f)
Despite *Frau* in the term, this is for male or female.

milf
Milf (f)

dirty whore
Dreckshure (f)

call girl
Callgirl (f)/Escort (f)

player
Checker (m)

two-pump chump
10-Sekunden-Tom (m)

horndog
geile Sau (f)

sadist
Sadist (m)

masochist
Masochist (m)

pervert
Perverser (m)

foot fetishist
Fuß-fetischist (m)

"MOVIE NIGHT"
DVD-ABEND/NETFLIX-ABEND/VIDEO-ABEND

"Video nights" are popular among small groups of German friends: beer, food, friends, and a flick; what could be better? But when you take into account that *Video-Abend* is also a euphemism for a sexy night at home, you may have to read between the lines the next time a "friend" invites you over for a movie night. Netflix and chill, anyone?

Hey baby, wanna watch a video?
Na Schätzchen, wollen wir ein Video gucken?

No, I'd rather make one ourselves!
Nee, ich drehe lieber unseren eigenen Heimporno!

Sounds like a great night to stay in!
Das wird aber ein schöner DVD-Abend sein!

---

rubber fetishist
Gummi-fetischist (m)

Peeping Tom
Spanner (m)

dominatrix
Domina (f)

dominator
Dominus (m)

CHAPTER 6

Smack Talk
Beschimpfen

Enemies
Feinde

There are varying types of jerks in this world, and knowing how to label and complain about them to your friends is an essential life skill. Equally important is knowing when someone might be complaining or talking trash about you, and knowing how to respond accordingly.

My **neighbors** shoot porno movies on their balcony.
*Meine **Nachbarn** drehen auf ihrem Balkon Porno Filme.*

My **landlord** is in the Russian mob.
*Mein **Vermieter** ist voll der Russenmafiatyp.*

My **boss** is a fuckin' drunk.
*Mein **Chef** ist voll der Säufer.*

My **ex** was making out with my brother!
*Mein(e) **Ex** hat mit meinem Bruder geknutscht!*

Ex is the same for male or female, but the adjective ending on the possessive pronoun shows you the person's gender.

My **mother-in-law** is completely schizo.
Mein Schwiegermonster ist echt durchgeknallt.
Literally, "monster-in-law."

Markus has owed me 100 Euros for months. What a **deadbeat**.
Markus schuldet mir seit Monaten 100 Euro. Voll der Gammler.

Tourists really piss me off!
Touristen nerven mich total!

Why are all **lawyers** so shitty?
Wieso sind alle Anwälte so fies?

Are German **politicians** crooked too?
Sind deutsche Politker auch so korrupt?

German **cops** don't really look intimidating.
Die deutschen Bullen sehen gar nicht so gefährlich aus.

Talkin' shit
Scheiße reden

When was the last time you went on for hours talking about what a nice person so-and-so is? Probably never. For some strange reason, humans just universally prefer to talk shit about each other. Why? Because humans are petty, that's why. So why not join the gossip-mongering fray by making fun of all the petty assholes out there?

Man, **I can't stand** those two.
Alda, die Beiden kann ich nicht aushalten.

What a complete **asshole**.
Was für ein Arschloch.

What an **idiot**!
Voll der Depp!

He is **full of shit**!
*Er hat nur **Luft im Sack**!*
Literally, "he has air in his balls."

She is always **talking shit** about us.
*Sie **redet nur Scheiße** über uns.*

Whoa, she's fuckin' **disgusting**.
*Bhoa, ist die voll **eklig**.*

She is a **stuck-up bitch**.
*Sie ist 'ne **hochnäsige Zicke**.*

He thinks he's so **special**.
*Er hält sich für was **Besonderes**.*

What a fucking **traitor**!
*Was für ein **Verräter**!*

You should see his Facebook page. Totally **creepy**.
*Du solltest sein Facebook profil sehen, echt **unheimlich**.*

That guy Holger makes me a little **nervous**.
*Der Holger macht mich etwas **nervös**.*

He's always just lurking around.
Er lungert einfach nur herum.

Stefanie's a total **kiss ass**.
*Stefanie spielt heute wieder **die Analraupe**.*
Literally, "acting like an anal caterpillar." Another option is the
Arschkriecher, or "one who crawls up your ass."

Watch out for him, he'll **totally fuck you over**!
*Pass mal auf, der **lässt dich voll im Stich**!*

He is a **total pain in the neck**.
*Er ist **voll die Nervensäge**.*

She'll talk your ear off!
Sie labert dir ein Kottelet ans Ohr!

THE HANDY DANDY LIST OF COMMON INSULTS
BELEIDIGUNGEN UND IHRE HANDHABUNG

Fucker
Penner (m)
Literally, "a bum," but you can also just call a guy a fucker and it carries the same weight.

Asshole
Arschloch (n)

Bitch
Zicke (f)

Sucker
Luscher (m)
This has the same weight as calling someone a wuss. *Waschlappen* (m) is a close relative, and means "dish rag."

Son-of-a-bitch
Arschmade (f)
Literally, "ass-maggot."

Cunt
Fotze (f)

Slut
Schlampe (f)

Whore
Hure (f)

Cocksucker
Schwunzlatscher (m)

Motherfucker
Motherfucker (m)

Piece of shit
Scheißkerl (m)

Shithead
Drecksau (f)
Literally, "a dirty pig."

Jackass
Arschgeige (f)
Literally, "ass-violin." Don't ask me why, but it is a hilarious and oddly effective insult.

Tool
Vollpfosten (m)
Literally, a post or a pole...a big one.

Don't let him fool you, he's **just blowin' smoke up yer ass!**
*Lass ihn dich nicht täuschen, der **bläst dir nur Puderzucker in den Hintern**!*
Literally, "blowing powdered sugar in your ass."

They used to be best friends until she found out the other one was a **total slut**.
*Die waren doch super befreundet, bis die eine es mitbekommen hat, dass die andere 'ne **miese Bumskuh** ist.*

She'll never be able to **make it up to me**.
*Die kann's mir nie **wieder gutmachen**.*

She can go fuck herself!
Sie kann sich verpissen!

He's a total **chump**!
*Er ist Voll die **Luftpumpe**!*

He's just a little **cry-baby**.
*Er ist echt nur ein **Tränentier**.*

Gettin' pissed
Sauer werden

Everybody's got their own threshold when it comes to containing their anger. Push them over it and they'll quickly lose their cool. Luckily, most Germans will tell you that you're pushing their buttons before they open a can of Teutonic whoop-ass on you, so it's only fair that you do the same in return. Here are some helpful words you'll need to let people know that you're starting to get pissed.

That stupid tourist....
Der dumme Tourist....

Just about everything....
Fast alles....

The way he/she looks....
Wie er/sie aussieht....

The way he/she talks....
Wie er/sie spricht....

Your attitude....
Deine Haltung....

> **bugs the hell outta me**
> *stört mich total*

> **gets under my skin**
> *geht mir unter die Haut*

> **drives me crazy!**
> *macht mich verrückt!*

> **is really annoying**
> *ist voll nervig*

> **pisses me off**
> *pisst mich an*

> **makes me so mad, I wanna puke**
> *ist zum Kotzen*

> **gets on my last nerve**
> *raubt mir den letzten Nerven*

> **drives me up the wall**
> *bringt mich auf die Palme*
> Literally, "drives me up the palm tree."

You're really bustin' my balls!
Du gehst mir auf den Sack!

I hate you.
Dich hasse ich.

Kiss my ass!
Leck mich doch am Arsch!

Piss off!
Verpiss dich!

Going postal
Durchdrehen

German is full of words for going nuts and losing your cool. Maybe it's the bitter winter weather. Maybe it's because Germany is surrounded by nine other countries that blame them for two world wars. Sometimes I think the only thing preventing Germans from going completely insane is the great beer, health care, social benefits, and four weeks of paid vacation a year. Whatever it is, Germans are more likely to express their insanity or anger in less violent ways than shooting up a post office. So, rather than getting violent, just talk about your frustrations and hash it out over a beer or four.

He spilled his beer on my new shoes and **I lost it.**
*Der hat Bier auf meine neuen Schuhe gekippt und ich bin einfach **abgedreht.***

When my girlfriend finds out, she's **gonna go postal.**
*Wenn meine Freundin es mitkriegt, wird sie **durchdrehen.***

I can't handle it anymore, I'm about to **flip out.**
*Ich kann's nicht mehr ertragen, ich **flippe gleich aus.***

Dude, **get a grip.**
*Äh man, **tick nicht ab.***

Are you **fucking nuts?**
***Spinnst Du** oder was?*

He's not playing with a full deck
Er hat nicht alle Tassen im Schrank.

She's **fucked in the head!**
*Sie hat **einen Dachschaden!***
Literally, "She's got **a damaged roof.**"

Totally mental
Am Blitz geleckt haben
Literally, "to lick a lightning bolt."

> That guy's totally **mental**!
> *Der hat wohl am **Blitz geleckt**!*

The shit has hit the fan.
Nun ist die Kacke am Dampfen.

Fighting
Kämpfen

Germany is pretty peaceful these days. The fallout from being responsible for two world wars kinda put the kibosh on public displays of aggression. But just because Germany isn't going to invade France anytime soon doesn't mean that there's no violence in the country. Though you don't really have to worry about UK-style soccer hooligan riots or L.A.-style drive-by shootings, politics can still get pretty heated. And if you get caught in the middle of a standoff between converging groups of left-wing anarcho-punks, right-wing skins, and the police, just watch for bricks aimed at your head.

Got a problem?
Ist was?

What about it?
Na und?

What's up with that shit?
Was soll der Scheiß?

SCHWARZENEGGER'S GUIDE TO FIGHTING
DAS SCHWARZENEGGER KAMPFLEXIKON

Punch
Schlag (m)

Kick
Tritt (m)

Karate chop
Karateschlag (m)

Roundhouse kick
Breitseite (f)

Choke hold
Würgegriff (m)

Uppercut
Uppercut (m)

Slap
Klaps (m)

Backhand
Rückhandschlag (m)

Headlock
Schwitzkasten (m)
Literally, "the sweat box."

Sucker punch
Suckerpunch (m)

Haymaker
Schwinger (m)

What do you want, **dipshit**?
*Was willste, Du **Pappnase**?*

OK, playtime's over.
Schluss mit lustig.

Go fuck yourself!
Fick dich ins Knie!
Literally, "go fuck yourself in the knee."

Hey, jerk-off!
Na, Du Wichser!

Shut your trap.
Halt die Klappe.

Shut the fuck up!
Halt's Maul!

What's with all the sexist bullshit?
Was soll diese sexistische Kackscheiße?

Quit your yelling!
Brüll nicht so 'rum!

I don't give a shit!
Ist mir doch scheißegal!

You worthless piece of shit!
Du mieses Miststück!

Want me to rearrange your face?
Sollte ich dir die Fresse polieren?
Literally, "polish your snout."

Beat it.
Geh kacken.
Literally, "go take a shit."

Get lost!
Zisch ab!

What, you chicken?
Wat, haste' Schiss?

Pussy!
Weichei!

Bring it on!
Na mach schon!

....

Avoiding violence
Gewalt vermeiden

German beat-downs are pretty rare. Most of the fights you'll encounter in Germany will be between two drunk guys and last all of about 30 seconds. But if you do happen to find yourself in a sticky situation, try out the following verbal gems to cool down some hotheads, break up a fight, or save yourself from getting stomped on.

Take it easy, man.
Eh man, locker bleiben.

Just take a deep breath.
Einfach tief einatmen.

Stop it.
Schluss damit.

Enough with the tough guy act.
Sei doch nicht so macho, eh.

Violence ain't the answer.
Gewalt ist keine Lösung.

It really ain't that big a deal, is it?
Ist alles doch pipifax, oder?

Dude, pull yourself together.
Mensch, reiß dich zusammen.

Bro, forget it.
Vergiss es, Digga.

This is really childish bullshit.
Das ist ja Kinderkacke.

Actually I'm a pacifist.
Eigentlich bin ich Pazifist.

Hey, cut that shit out.
Hey, hör auf mit dem Scheiß.

I'd rather not get involved.
Ich misch mich lieber nicht ein.

Fuck this, I'm callin' the cops.
Scheiß drauf, ich hol' die Bullen.

It's all just water under the bridge.
Ist doch Schnee von gestern.
Literally, "it's just snow from yesterday," meaning it's already melted away.

Let's wipe the slate clean.
Schwamm drüber.
Literally, "let's sponge it off."

....

The cops
Die Bullen

As the son of a retired sheriff, I have nothing but respect for police. But German cops can be kind of a joke. In smaller towns, they don't do much except hang around shopping centers, drive around in VW Golf and Passat cop cars, and look bored. If it weren't for the guns, they'd almost look like they were going to pick their kids up from soccer practice. The cops in Bavaria can be real dicks, though. My friend once got stopped in a park in Munich because she was using a mirror to check her contact lens. Munich's finest thought she was sniffing coke and went on a whole "not in my town, blah, blah, blah" rant.

Riot cops are another story. They stand guard at all the political demonstrations, train stations, and soccer matches, and they just wait for an excuse to run you over in their "green and white party bus," or hose you down with water cannons.

Fuckin' cops.
Scheiß Bullen.

Here come(s) the....
Hier kommt/kommen....

> **police**
> *Polizei (f)*
>
> **popo**
> *Polente (f)*
>
> **pigs**
> *Bullen (pl)*
>
> **occifer**
> *Pozelei (f)*
> A pun on *Polizei*. Like saying, "Howdy Occifer!"
>
> **fuzz**
> *Buletten (f)*

That jerk's an **undercover cop**.
*Der Spacken da ist 'n **Zivilbulle**.*

The **Paddy Wagon**'s comin'.
*Der **Grün-weiße Party Bus** kommt.*
Most cop cars are green and white, and so is the bus they haul your ass away in.

Put that shit away.
Weg mit dem Scheiß.

Dude, let's bail.
Eh, lass uns vom Acker.
Literally, "let's get off the field."

They just ran off.
Sie sind einfach abgehauen.

Don't say shit.
Schnauze!
Literally, "snout."

Dude, don't snitch.
Hey Digga, nicht verpfeifen.

They'll throw your ass in the clink for that.
Dafür kommste in den Knast.

If you're brave enough to taunt the cops with your new anarchist friends, try out the following German classics. But be careful, cuz German cops can throw your ass in jail just for making fun of them. The crime is called *Amtsbeleidigung* (insulting the officer) and can land you in the clink. Seriously.

Ficken Bullen nicht Kühe?
Don't bulls fuck cows?
This is kinda like asking "Do you smell bacon?" in front of a cop in the States.

A.C.A.B./F.D.P.
All Cops Are Bastards/Fuck da' Police
Both are favorite chants at riots and demonstrations.

CHAPTER 7

Pop Culture & Technology
Popkultur & Technologie

Unlike in France, where 40 percent of music played on radio stations has to be French, Germany doesn't have a bunch of laws that try to protect their cultural heritage. As a result, American pop culture has always muscled in on everyday German life. Some people hate it, some people love it, but it appears to be here to stay. So don't be surprised when you flip on the radio and hear loads of English language artists that are popular in the states or Britain, or you catch Mr. T pitying the fool in German on *Das A-Team* while channel surfing.

Music
Mucke

Are you into...?
Stehst Du auf...?

What's the deal with...?
Was soll das eigentlich mit...?

...is totally awesome.
...ist echt der Hammer.
Literally, "the hammer."

...is for kids.
...ist für den Kindergarten.

...is for losers.
...ist für Loser.

I wanna hear some...
Ich will etwas...hören.

Pop

German pop is just as mainstream and vanilla as it is the world over. The charts are filled with American or international pop hits, though Germany does have its own pop groups. You'll likely hear something from Xavier Naidoo, Silbermond, Glasperlenspiel, or ICH + ICH in between songs from Justin Bieber, Rihanna, or Coldplay.

Rock and Roll

No matter where you go, rock is rock.

Krautrock

Weird, psychedelic progressive rock that got popular in the '60s and '70s in West Germany. Kraftwerk is likely a band you've heard of, but Can, Tangerine Dream, and Neu! are three *Krautrock* groups definitely worth looking into.

Ostrock

East Germany's answer to *Krautrock*, but not exclusively for hippies. City, Karat, Silly, and Puhdys are the heavy hitters of *Ostrock*, and although still way more popular among former citizens of East Germany, they were able to keep their audiences and gain new Western fans following the fall of the wall.

Punk

Everything from really hard-core political punk like Dritte Wahl and Slime to fun, party punk like Die Ärtzte and the original German party punks, Die Toten Hosen.

Boy Groups

Although American groups dominate this category (which is nothing to be proud of), Germans have a strong front-runner with Tokio Hotel. Imagine if N'Sync and a Japanese pop group combined. Of course, they see themselves as more of a rock band than a *Boy Group*, and are constantly "evolving."

Schlager

This originated as jazz-like film music in the '20s and '30s but stopped being cool in the '60s. It doesn't even sound good when you're drunk—except for Heino, a one-man guitar-playing demon. He looks like a walleyed, blonde version of Roy Orbison and sounds like Pat Boone with a big set of balls. Heino's the shit. Of course, almost every German has a favorite *Schlager* song, and is likely to break into song the next time you're out with them at any festival, so you should find your own favorite *Schlager*.

Volksmusik

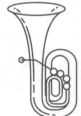

Literally, "the music of the people," it consists of traditional German music, like the *Oompah* brass bands at Oktoberfest, or a crappy, modern-day synthesized version thereof. It's mostly ballads about the forest and mountains. *Omas* and *Opas* love this shit.

Rap/Hip-hop

American rappers are popular, but Hamburg and Berlin are the capitals of German hip-hop, with dozens of big-name rappers. Die Fantastischen Vier are like the German Beastie Boys, and they really paved the way for German Hip Hop.

Black Music

As you might guess, this is pretty much music by black people. The charts cover everything from rap to R&B and soul as well as reggae. The name isn't meant to be derogatory, but I can't help but cringe every time I'm in a record store and see the label.

Dark Wave

A favorite of German Goth kids, extra spooky and extra weird.

Industrial

Einstürzende Neubauten are the godfathers of industrial music, which is fitting, seeing that their name translates to "collapsing new buildings." No one else can make a power saw sound like sweet music quite the way these guys do.

Electronic

Kraftwerk were the original pioneers of German electronic music, but the genre has since expanded to include everything from house to experimental to techno. There are a lot of good German electronic bands and a lot of shitty ones, too. Le Rok is one of the awesome ones. Check them out.

Neue deutsche Welle (NDW)

Meaning "New German Wave." Remember Falco, Peter Schilling, and Nena? NDW is '80s music that made it cool again for bands to sing in German. Like British New Wave, there are both "underground" and "pop" versions in Germany, too. All of it still kicks ass and is still pretty popular in clubs. Your date will dig it if you get out and dance whenever someone spins 99 Luftballons.

Indie

Largely based around the '80s and '90s phenomenon of the *Hamburger Schule*, meaning the "Hamburg School." German indie rock comes from all over the country but is especially synonymous with Hamburg, similar to the way that grunge was synonymous with Seattle back in the '90s. Die Sterne, Blumfeld, Tocotronic, and even the punk band *Die Goldenen Zitronen* are a few Hamburg School bands that rocked the Kiez.

"Neue" neue deutsche Welle

Bands like Spillsbury, Tomte, Sportfreunde Stiller, and Kettcar are the "new" New German Wave. Take the best of *Hamburger Schule* and *NDW* and you've got something equivalent to retro-'80s music with German lyrics.

Neue deutsche Härte

Rammstein introduced the U.S. to the genre that translates to *"New German Hardness."* It's also referred to as *Tanzmetall,* or "dance metal," which is, well, metal you can dance to.

TV and movies
Film und Fernsehen

Germans are bombarded with tons of American TV shows and movies. Instead of subtitling these shows, voice actors are hired to dub all the dialogue. It's kinda funny at first, but then it's really sad when you realize that the same voiceover actor who does John Travolta also does Bruce Lee. Of course, as with all things in the 21st century, the Internet has done a lot to break down this particular part of the language barrier. Most of your friends will either stream or download shows from abroad, and they're often still in the original language. Of course, the Germans do have their own TV shows, as well as the German versions of international franchises.

Don't you guys ever watch German shows?
Schaut ihr keine deutschen Sendungen?

Let's watch...
Gucken wir....

...is the best show on TV.
...ist die geilste Sendung.

Big Brother

Yeah, Germany has a version of this show, too. The only thing that makes it remotely cooler than the U.S. version is that it can show nudity. Nothing beats spying on naked people on CCTV.

Ich bin ein Star – Holt mich hier raus!

Based on the British TV show of the same name (*I'm a Star, Get Me Out of Here!*), this "reality" show is mostly referred to as *Dschungelcamp, or* "The Jungle Camp." For over a decade, the producers have stuck nearly a dozen well-known and not-so-well-known stars in a camp in the Australian Outback, and we watch what happens.

Wetten Dass...?

This German TV classic (whose English name is *Wanna Bet?*) is sadly off the air. It was a special, live TV event that aired several times a year from different German (or sometimes Austrian or Swiss) cities, and offered everyday contestants the chance to perform simple tasks in an odd and entertaining manner. Celebrity guests would bet on whether the contestant could complete the task. It was a mindless favorite, and everyone remembers when Mark Kälin was able to blow up three condoms using his nose!

Deutschland Sucht den Superstar (DSDS)

The Germanic version of *American Idol.* The contestants here are just as "talented" as they are in America.

Julia Leischik Sucht: Bitte Melde Dich

This weird classic (whose English name is *Julia Leischik is Searching: Please Get in Touch*) is sort of like an *America's Most Wanted*, but instead of serial killers and child molesters, they are searching for lost relatives or missing people, with the hope that they'll see the show and "Get in Touch."

Tatort
On air for nearly 50 years, this is the classic German cop show that just about everyone watches, even if they don't admit it. *CSI* is for chumps; it's all about *Tatort*.

Polizeruf-110
Cop shows were oddly popular in the former East Germany, and this one managed to outlive the fall of the Berlin Wall and gain popularity with Germans on both sides.

Der Tatortreiniger
Solving actual crimes takes a backseat in this wildly popular comedy series that follows the misadventures of Schotty, the janitor, whose specialty is cleaning up the nasty leftovers of a crime scene, finding the perfect combination between humor and uncomfortable subject matter.

Lindenstraße
This soap opera, or *Telenovelle,* about a bunch of neighbors living in Munich has been on since the Cold War. It's set in Munich, but is actually filmed in Köln. The show set off an uproar in 1990 when it showed the first gay kiss on prime-time German TV.

Gute Zeiten, Schlechte Zeiten
Literally, "Good Times, Bad Times." This classic *Telenovelle* for teens has been on TV for over 25 years. Following an ever-evolving cast of young Berliners, the series' 6000+ episodes have introduced young audiences to serious social topics like rape, drugs, crime, incest, cancer, and mental illness.

Schlag den Raab
Moderator Stefan Raab gained fame as the host of the late-night comedy show, *TV TOTAL*. His unique brand

of humor mocked other shows and always had special guests to help out. In this spin-off, a challenger competes against Raab for the chance to win a million Euros. With its odd challenges, it was sorta like a Japanese game show, but less hokey. Sadly, both this show and its predecessor are now off the air.

Richterin Barbara Salesch

The "German Judge Judy" is less abrasive, but she still has red hair and annoys everyone who doesn't adore her. There are like 10 different German court TV shows, all of which provide not only a frightening look into the underbelly of German society, but are good for a laugh too.

Eurovision Song Contest

This is like the World Cup for European pop music. Every year since 1956, each European country submits their contender for the best pop song, and everyone turns on the tube to watch and vote for their favorite singer. Germany has only won twice, first with Nicole (1982), and then with Lena in 2010. In 2014, Austria's Tom Neuwirth made waves when he appeared as the bearded drag queen alter-ego "Conchita Wurst" to push the contest's boundaries, and won.

Humor
Humor

Like British cuisine or French military, German humor sounds like a contradiction. Nothing could be further from the truth. Germans are hilarious. Their diverse regional customs and dialects make for a lot of cultural misunderstandings, and thus serious comedic fodder. German comics capitalize on this, making fun of everybody around, and usually in their local dialects. Of course, much of the humor and jokes don't really translate well, so the more you get comfortable with the language, the more you can enjoy a good laugh with your friends.

Schadenfreude (f)

Much of German humor focuses on people poking fun at themselves, and others. Who else but the Germans could have a term that translates as "malicious joy"? This is all about laughing at the pain and misfortune of others.

Kabarett (n)

Kabarett is the specific genre of scathing political and social satire. It's often stated that German humor needs a target, and these satirists, or *Kabarettisten*, take a darkly comedic and cynical look at society. They often take it very seriously.

German comedy
Deutsche Komiker

Loriot

Loriot is the absolute giant of classic German comedy. His sketches and cartoons exploited *Schadenfreude* to its fullest. Some think of him as Germany's answer to Monty Python, but he's way cooler because he was actually a real person.

Harald Schmidt

Germany's version of Letterman or Leno got some serious laughs (and shit) by poking fun at Hitler on national television.

Studio Braun

Hamburg's answer to the *Jerky Boys*. This comedy troupe's weird prank calls range from a telemarketer offering discount wigs to grandmas to a guy getting groped by his pet Sasquatch. Trust me, they're hilarious. The members also created FRAKTUS, Germany's *Krautrock* answer to Spinal Tap, complete with their own film and a series of live shows.

JOKES
WITZE

Witz means "joke," and if you stick -*witz* at the end of your favorite subject, you've just invented a whole new genre of jokes.

Hey, you know any…?
Sag mal, kennste einige…?

All right, enough of the stupid…
Also, die blöden…reichen mir schon.

…are the funniest.
…sind voll lustig.

Hey, have you guys heard this one yet?
Na, habt ihr diesen schon gehört?

Was that meant to be funny?
Sollte das ein Witz sein?

Is there a **punchline**?
*Gibt's 'ne **Pointe**?*

Titanic
Germany's second largest satire magazine is certainly the funniest, and most confrontational. Comparing *Titanic* to *The Onion* is like comparing a nuclear weapon with a water pistol. *Titanic*'s cover images have lampooned everyone from Hitler to every recent German chancellor to the Pope! The magazine is so dedicated that the editors even founded their own political party, *Die Partei* (The Party), and the former Editor-in-Chief won a seat in the European Parliament!

Bully
A stand-up and sketch comedian from Munich who got huge with his TV show *Bullyparade*, where he makes fun of all things Bavarian and creates classic comedy sketches, like his sweetly gay-themed *Star Trek/ German Love Boat* parody, *Unser (T) Raumschiff*.

Ausbilder Schmidt

Is he a comic or a drill sergeant? Ausbuilder Schmidt makes Triumph the insult comic dog look like the little Chihuahua from those Taco Bell commercials. I'm not sure if my side hurts from all the laughing or the sit-ups he made me do.

Dieter Nuhr

A wildly popular but somewhat controversial *Kabarettist*, known for his no-holds-barred approach to social critique and commentary, Nuhr sort of epitomizes the term *nörgeln*, or to grumble or gripe. It was even the name of one of his shows— *Nuhr am Nörgeln*, which means "Nuhr is griping." Since his last name is pronounced just like the German word *nur*, which means "only," the title is a pun, with the double meaning of "Only Griping."

Jan Böhmermann

As a satirist, author, radio and TV host, and comedian, Böhmermann has held almost every job in entertainment. Most notably, he's the host of the weekly satirical talk show *Neo Magazin Royale*, which is like an even more satirical *The Daily Show*. He really got himself into hot water for his scathing political commentary directed at Turkish president Erdogan.

Atze Schröder

Comedian Hubertus Albers' alter-ego is Germany's answer to Andrew Dice Clay, only not as sexist or dumb, and is like a thousand times funnier. Atze is a lovable, womanizing kiosk owner from the heart of industrial Germany, the Ruhrpott, and is the real blue-collar deal. Instead of rocking the leather jacket and pompadour, Schröder sports a cheesy perm and porno shades.

Cindy aus Marzahn (Ilka Bessin)

Sort of a cross between Atze Schröder and Roseanne Barr, Cindy aus Marzahn is a caricature of the typical *Ossi*. In her trademark heavy make-up and pink track suit, Cindy aus Marzahn is the sweetly dumpy, working-class *Proll* alter ego of one of Germany's highest paid female comedians, Ilka Bessin, known for her sarcastic, self-deprecating, and often stereotypically low-brow observational humor.

Fashion
Mode

When it comes to German fashion, most people think of guys in funny hats wearing socks with sandals. Of course, modern Germans look nothing like that. Berlin and Düsseldorf are major European fashion centers, and younger Germans, especially in the bigger cities, are always up on the latest styles and love anything new and different. More often than not, their fashion blows away anything from the States. And while the old Cold War myth about Germans selling a kidney for a pair of blue jeans died out with online shopping, you may still make some new friends by trading your Abercrombie T-shirt for some weird-ass Euro shoes.

The scene
Szene (f)

Clothes
Klamotten (pl)

I'm into gals/dudes who dress....
Ich stehe auf Mädchen/Typen, die...Klamotten tragen.

I only wear...clothes.
Ich trage nur...Klamotten

I'm totally....
Ich bin voll....

> **sporty**
> *sportlich*

Like you just came from the gym, but all stylish and put together, not gross and sweaty.

preppy
edel
Usually white sneakers, insanely expensive jeans, and Polo shirts.

business
amtlich/business
For some reason, all German businessmen have these weird blue dress shirts that they wear with everything.

punk/emo
punk/emo
Kinda like Hot Topic pop-punk style. These are the teddy bears of punk rock, and just about as threatening.

hipster/indie rock
indie
Skinny, pale dudes in track jackets with tight T-shirts, corduroy jeans, and old Adidas sneakers are the standard. For some reason, German indie kids aren't as annoying as American ones.

rockabilly
oldschool
Basically rockabilly gals and greaser guys, but without the same redneck vibe you get at a Mike Ness show. Lots of jeans and black T-shirts and tattoos. Like in the states, it's really popular with older punkers who don't wanna grow up.

goth
gothic
The standard uniform of the *Grufti* and Dark Wave crowd. Think spooky girls with coffin purses to scary guys who look like the walking dead, ready to eat your soul.

skinhead
skin/oi

A skinhead's trademark look is polo shirts with boots, suspenders, jeans, and, of course, a shaved head. Like in the States, most *Oi* kids aren't racist and are usually pretty cool. But be on the lookout, cuz there are still some right-wing skins in Germany who might want to kick your ass for no reason. Fortunately, they are few and far between.

vintage
second-hand/vintage

Not crap from the Salvation Army, but actually good vintage threads. If you think your worn-out Members Only jacket is cool, the average German *Secondhandladen* (vintage store) will blow you away. Schrader is an amazing store that sells vintage threads by the kilo, literally.

mainstream
streetwear

This is the generic term for youth fashions. Lots of American influence, and pretty boring to look at.

skater
skater

As mainstream as this style's become, you may be surprised when you see a skater kid who actually owns and rides a skateboard. But in just about every German city there are still tons of skaters who brave the cobblestone streets with their boards and 90-Euro Vans "Old Skool"shoes.

hip-hop
hiphop

These guys follow the trends in America, but tend to throw their own Euro flair into the mix.

raver
techno/raver/EDM

You can usually spot their rubber pants, pink hair, platform shoes, space-age backpacks, and giant goggles from across the train station. They often look like anime characters who just huffed a bunch of Xanax, but to each their own.

Your outfit looks really....
Dein Outfit ist echt....

cute
hübsch

pretty
schön

stylish
modisch

expensive
teuer

cheap
billig

stupid
blöd

ridiculous
bescheuert

cheesy
kitschig

awesome
der Hammer
Literally, "the hammer."

cool
geil

out-dated
out

He/She....
Er/Sie....

is kinda tan
ist etwas gebräunt

is kinda pale
ist etwas blass

is hip
ist im Trend

is clueless when it comes to fashion
hat keine Ahnung von Mode

is popular with the guys/girls
beliebt bei den Jungs/Mädels

is a pretty girl
ist ein schönes Mädchen

is a handsome guy
ist ein attraktiver Kerl

looks like a model
ist voll Modelmäßig

looks like a bum
sieht aus wie ein Penner

is a total nerd
ist echt nerdmäßig

Talking tech
Fachjargon

Even if you're not a tech-nerd, you've likely got a smart-phone and a computer. Don't be worried about trying to use them in Germany. Since most high-tech devices have chargers that can handle multiple voltages, you will likely only need an adapter to fit the German outlets. If your smartphone takes a SIM card, you're probably in the clear and can just buy a prepaid card and pop it in. Watch out, however, as plans can be really expensive, especially with data. Luckily for you, tech-talk uses terms that are taken straight from English, so it will be pretty easy when you need to explain what happened to your *Handy*.

Laptop
Laptop (m)

Desktop computer
Desktop-rechner (m)

Flat-screen monitor
Flachbildschirm (m)

Touch-screen monitor
Touchscreen (m)

Cell phone
Handy (n)

Smartphone
Smartphone (n)

Prepaid card
Prepaid Karte (f)

Sim card
Sim-Karte (f)

Flat-rate
Flatrate (f)

Charger
Ladegerät (n)

Hashtag
Hashtag (m)

App
App (f)

Mouse
Maus (f)

Attachment (document, etc.)
Anhang (m)

Connection/port
Anschluss (m)

Reception
Empfang (m)

To upload
Hochladen

To download
Herunterladen

To install
Installieren

To uninstall
Deinstallieren

To delete
Löschen

To swipe
Wischen

To scroll
Scrollen

To save (data, telephone number, etc.)
Speichern

To upgrade
Upgraden

Text message
SMS (f)

To send a text message
SMSen (pronounced like "zimzen") / *Texten*

Typo
Tippfehler (m)

Can I borrow your **cellphone charger**?
*Kannst Du mir dein **Handy-Ladegerät** leihen?*

I'm not getting any **cell reception** out here, let's bounce.
*Hier kriege ich null **Empfang**, lass uns abhauen.*

Coffee shops that don't offer **free wifi** are bullshit.
*Café's ohne **gratis W-lan Hotspots** sind zum Kotzen.*

Who actually pays for **apps** these days?
*Wer zahlt den für **Apps**?*

Just text me, I never pick up the phone.
***Schick mir einfach eine SMS**, ich geh nie ans Telefon.*

This is **taking way too long** to download!
*Dieser Download **dauert echt zu lange**!*

I'm taking a **break from social media** for a while.
*Ich mache gerade eine **Facebook-Pause**.*

It's impossible to check even my emails with this **slow-ass laptop**!
*Mit meinem **lahmarschigen Laptop** kann ich kaum meine E-mails checken!*

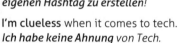

What's your **email address**?
*Wie ist deine **E-Mail-Adresse**?*

My Grandma **tried to create her own hashtag** the other day!
*Neulich hat meine Oma **versucht ihren eigenen Hashtag zu erstellen**!*

I'm clueless when it comes to tech.
***Ich habe keine Ahnung** von Tech.*

What's the deal with Uber and Lyft in Germany?
***Was ist los mit** Uber und Lyft in Deutschland?*

Germany's labor laws and restrictions have been problematic for both companies. There are alternative providers for taxis, etc., that work in accordance with these laws and are successful. Uber is present in some larger cities, but you're essentially using the service to order a licensed taxi.

I finally **upgraded** my phone!
*Endlich habe ich habe mein Handy **geupgraded**!*

Are you into Apple or Android?
***Stehst Du auf** Apple oder Android?*

Detlev is a freak, I **had to block** him on Instagram and Facebook.
*Detlev ist voll der Spacko, den habe ich auf Instagram und Facebook **blockieren müssen**.*

I accidentally **deleted** all of my contacts from my phone.
*Aus Versehen habe ich meine Kontakte vom Handy **gelöscht**.*

Nerding out
Nerdheit

In Germany, nerds aren't really social outcasts. Like a lot of nerds, German ones are just hard-core fired up about whatever they're into. But for some strange reason, German nerds are especially into collecting stuff. It's likely due to that stereotypically German trait of being overly precise and orderly that carries over into their obsessions. Sometimes they're overtly proud of their collections, and sometimes they hide them like dirty little secrets.

To collect
Sammeln

What do you collect?
Was sammelst Du?

He's a total....
Er ist ein echter....

> **nerd**
> *Nerd (m)*

> **collector nerd**
> *Sammler-nerd*

> **record nerd**
> *Platten-nerd*

> **comic book nerd**
> *Comic-nerd*

> **computer nerd**
> *Computer-nerd*

He's/She's kinda nerdy.
*Er/Sie ist etwas **Nerd-mäßig**.*

I'm proud to be a nerd.
Ich bin stolz, Nerd zu sein.

All my best friends are nerds.
Alle meine Kumpels sind Nerds.

COOL, MAN!
GEIL, ALDA!

Although you've likely heard it used in the classroom setting as "cool!" you've quickly come to learn through this book that *Geil* also means horny. How and when you use the term dictates it's meaning. If you're really excited about something, or think it's really cool, try mixing a few over-the-top versions of Geil into your ever-expanding vocabulary. Remember, it's up to you to be the first one to invent the newest incarnation of Geil, so get to it.

Cool!
Geil!

Totally cool!
Voll geil!

Insanely cool!
Mega geil!

Fuckin' cool!
Affengeil!
Literally, "ape cool."

Insanely fuckin' cool!
Oberaffengeil!

Totally sick!
Krass!

Uncontrollably cool!
Echt pornös!

Wow, Germans are **a bunch of nerds**.
*Die Deutschen sind ein echt **nerd-mäßiges Volk**.*

I just don't get all the **nerdiness**.
*Diese **Nerdheit** verstehe ich nicht.*

I'm **totally into** nerds.
*Ich bin **echt heiß auf** Nerds.*

Can I show you my **stamp collection**?
*Darf ich dir noch meine **Briefmarkensammlung** zeigen?*

Not only one of the nerdiest things a German can ask you, it's also a classic, clichéd German pickup line that's really just an invitation to hop into the sack.

My **collection of**...is way cooler than yours.
*Meine...**Sammlung** ist viel cooler als deine.*

Ü-eiersammlung

Tons of Germans collect the little toys that come in *Überraschungseier*, or little chocolate eggs with a prize. Some of the toys are worth some serious Euros. I knew a dude who paid for his year abroad when he sold his collection. But don't even think of trying to bring these into the U.S. Their importation has been banned.

Telefonkarten

Another huge collectible item is used phone cards. I shit you not.

Bierdeckel

It seems almost a no-brainer that there's a community of beer coaster collectors. I've even seen someone make furniture out of these cardboard wonders.

Hörspiele

Tapes and records of children's stories. *TKKG* and *Die drei Fragezeichen* are childhood classics that are great to fall asleep to.

Comics, cartoons, and cult icons
Comics, Zeichentrickfilme, und Kultfiguren

I think the stress of being blamed for two world wars has forced some Germans to escape reality by regressing into the safety of their childhood. Lots of them surround themselves with kiddy-kitsch for comfort. Sometimes it's subtle, like a cutesy figurine on their desk or

a few comics tucked away by their bed. Other times it's batshit-crazy, like people who wear embroidered denim Looney Tunes shirts and only have sex in bunny costumes. In moderation, this fondness for all things childish is cool, but watch out for the crazies.

Comics
Comics (pl)

The Little Asshole
Das kleine Arschloch

Probably the most popular German comic strip. *The Little Asshole* is a nearsighted kid who runs around naked and insults everyone under the sun. The artist Walter Moers is also responsible for *Der Alte Sack* (the Old Grouch: an embittered old man in a wheelchair), *Adolf, die Nazisau* (Adolf, the Nazi-pig: an absurd parody of Hitler, who, after 50 years of hiding in Berlin sewers, resurfaces in modern Germany) and *Käpt'n Blaubär* (see below).

EAST GERMAN NOSTALGIA
OSTALGIE

Ostalgie is a specific word for nostalgia for all things East German (as in from the former GDR). While some older Germans see it as an inappropriate fixation on an oppressive regime, others are just clinging to the good times they had as kids. Politics aside, it's really just a marketing term to cash in on T-shirts and childhood kitsch with old GDR brands and pop culture figures.

Aside from the Stasi, the Wall, and the Russians, the GDR wasn't all that bad, was it?
Abgesehen von der Stasi, der Mauer, und den Russen, war die DDR nicht so schlimm, oder?

Diddl
Diddl

This horribly annoying, cutesy comic strip mouse is especially popular with girls and lonely women. If someone you meet has anything *Diddl*-related, watch out, you might just get a birthday card with him on it.

Cartoons
Zeichentrickfilme (pl)

Kids shows
Kindersendungen (pl)

The Show with the Mouse
Die Sendung mit der Maus

Like a cross between Saturday morning cartoons and the Discovery Channel for kids. The cartoon mouse, along with his friends Elephant and Duck, are German icons and can be found on everything from pajamas and bedsheets to notebooks and coffee mugs.

Dandylion
Löwenzahn

The host Peter Lustig is the German Mr. Rogers, but he lives in a gypsy-like caravan and wears farmer overalls. Despite the immense possibility of his being creepy, he's not. Really, he's not.

Maja the Bee
Die Biene Maja

This cartoon from the '70s doesn't get old, at least not if you watched it when you were a kid. She's a cute bee who's always screwing something up and then getting herself out of a jam.

The Little Sandman
Das Sandmännchen

A hit kids' show from the former GDR. The Sandman stars in little stop-motion animation shorts that are shown before kids go to sleep. Get it? The Sandman puts them to sleep. He's got friends, too, like Pittiplatsch, a weird pygmy elf thing, and Schnatterinchen the duck.

Capt'n Bluebear
Käpt'n Blaubär

An old sea captain, who happens to be a blue bear, tells his grandkids ridiculous stories about his adventures. There's a little double entendre going on with some inside jokes for adults, kinda like *Pee Wee's Playhouse* without the public masturbation and felonies.

Bernd, the Loaf of Bread
Bernd das Brot

Bernd is the gloomy, ill-tempered, self-deprecating mascot of the German kid's TV channel Ki.Ka (sort of like

PBS kids), whose "show" originally ran in a loop during the station's late-night "off hours." He quickly became a cult favorite among German adults, and adorns everything from coffee mugs to T-shirts and stationary.

CHAPTER 8

Sports & Games
Sport & Spiele

Despite Germany's cultural and linguistic differences, the one thing that brings them all together is their love of sports. Germans love just about every sport on the planet, though soccer, basketball, handball, formula 1, and cycling are especially high on their list.

In a weird twist of Germanic irony, the one sport universally loved by all Germans, *Fußball*, is the very thing that leads to some serious inter-German rivalry. At soccer games, German fan loyalty puts your average Yankee fan to shame. Visiting fans arrive at matches more like invading armies than simple rivals. I once got stuck in a train station where hordes of Schalke 04 fans faced off with fans from Bayern München, and I thought I was gonna get trampled to death.

Sports
Sport

Do you like to play....
Spielst Du gern....

I wanna play....
Ich will...spielen.

> **ice hockey**
> *Eishockey*

> **basketball**
> *Basketball*

> **tennis**
> *Tennis*

> **handball**
> *Handball*
> Olympic handball, which is played like soccer with your hands. It's pretty popular.

> **formula 1**
> *Formel eins*

> **American football**
> *Football*

> **soccer**
> *Fußball*
> This is, hands down, the number 1 sport in Germany.

Let's watch....
Lass uns...gucken.

> **something else**
> *was anderes*

> **the sports news**
> *die Sportschau*
> Germany's equivalent of Sports Center.

Why are the Germans so crazy about soccer?
Warum sind die Deutschen verrückt nach Fußball?

Which...do you like?
Welche...magst Du?

> **types of sports**
> *Sportarten (pl)*
>
> **teams**
> *Mannschaften (pl)*
>
> **players**
> *Spieler (pl)*

Weird world of sports
Außergewöhnliche Sportarten

The Germans like to drink beer. A lot of it. This might explain why some of the following bizarre sports caught on in Germany.

So, I've never heard of....
Von...habe ich nie gehört.

Do you guys really play....
Spielt ihr eigentlich...?

> ### Aquaball
> It's kinda like a weird combination of soccer and water polo, only you're playing in a kiddy pool and the kids mock you.
>
> ### Autoball
> Invented by comedian Stefan Raab (who also introduced the world to Wok-sledding), it's basically demolition derby mixed with soccer.

Klootschießen

The key to "road bowling," otherwise known as "Ostfriesland's National Sport," is pretty simple. Find a long stretch of road, a couple of wooden balls, and some bored northern Germans. It's like a combination relay race/shot put. Teams compete for distance by chucking the ball as far as they can, and the next teammate starts where the ball lands.

Hakeln

This is Bavarian beerhall tug-of-war with fingers. Seated across from each other at a massive wooden table, each *Hakler* (roughly translates as "hooker") locks, or rather "hooks," his finger onto a little rope. Pull the other guy over the table and you win. Just don't spill your beer.

Jugger

Who else but the Germans would catch on to a weird postapocalyptic game taken from a sci-fi movie? OK, maybe the Japanese, but then it would involve giant robots and be televised. *Jugger*, however, is decidedly uncool. It's like soccer and lacrosse combined with live-action role-playing (LARPING), foam weapons, and a dog skull made of rubber for the ball.

Kegeln

This is like 10th-century bowling. You use nine small pins and a small ball without holes. Bowling alleys are everywhere in Germany, but the *Kegelbahn* is really where it's at.

Prellball

Kinda like volleyball, except the net is only about 12 inches high and you have to bounce the ball on your side over the net and hope the other team doesn't send it back. It looks really lame, in case you were wondering.

Rhönradturnen

You know the wheel that clowns roll around in at the circus? It isn't just a stupid trick; it's wheel gymnastics!

Unterwasserrugby

Underwater rugby: yep, exactly what it sounds like.

Schleuderball

Literally, "sling ball." How else can you describe a game where you have to sling a horsehair-filled ball by its handle at the other team's goal?

Bar games
Kneipensport

Bars aren't much more than the last resort to find love or a place to drown your sorrows. Most Germans prefer to get sloshed in a pub-like *Kneipe*, where they can also challenge their friends to useless games of "skill."

Wanna play some...?
Wollen wir mal...?

...is the shit.
...ist der Hammer.

...isn't really my thing.
...ist nicht mein Ding.

Do you know how to play...?
Kannst Du...?

cards
Karten spielen
Skat is the national card game of Germany. It's like bridge with a smaller deck and is more confusing if you're drunk. I think only old people really get it.

dice
Knobeln
Kinda like Yahtzee, but less nerdy and includes way more trash talk. People play this for hours, usually for drinks.

pool
Billiard spielen

ping-pong
Tischtennis spielen

darts
Dart spielen

pinball
Flippern

bowling
Bowlen

foosball
Kickern

This is huge in almost every *Kneipe*. Foosball gets its name from *Fußball*. If you think you're good at it just because you can beat everyone in your dorm, wait until you play the Germans. They're demons at *Kickern*.

table soccer
Tipp-Kick spielen

Not foosball, but a hugely popular and a kinda dorky/kinda cool game where two opponents face off on a table-top felt field with two little soccer player figures. Basically, you just push the button on your player's head and he kicks a black and white octagonal ball at a little goal. They've even got national *Tipp-Kick spielen* tournaments for serious nerds.

Outdoor recreation
Freiluftsport

As you've likely learned from the little "cultural focus" sections from just about every German textbook, Germans are totally into the outdoors. Any chance they have to get in tune with nature, they jump at. Something that was most definitely missing from your textbook is that, for whatever reason, lots of Germans just love being outside and naked—try not to stare. An important tip for first-timers, watch out when it comes to hanging out at the beach, or in the park in the summer.

Wanna go...?
Wollen wir...?

sun bathing
sonnenbaden

to the nude beach
zum FKK Strand
Stands for *Freikörperkultur*, or "free body culture," and it ain't all that sexy.

hiking
wandern

wakeboarding
wakeboarden

rock climbing
klettern

kayaking
Kajak fahren

canoeing
paddeln

mountain biking
Mountainbike fahren

on a bike tour
eine Radtour machen

camping
zelten

Camping in Germany is kind of a pain. You can't camp in the wild, so lots of people spend the summers at official campsites on the beaches in the north, in the Alps, or at some lakes. If you're feeling adventurous, plenty of farmers are willing to let you stay on their land as long as you clean up after yourself, so make sure you take your empties with you.

to an open festival
zum Open-air gehen

Kinda like camping, only with 20,000 punkers, emos, or metal kids, lots of loud music, drinking, and of course, mud. The Wacken Open Air festival, or WOA, is not only Germany's largest open-air Metal festival, it's the largest in the world. For days in August, metal fans from all over the world descend on the sleepy farming village of Wacken to celebrate all things metal, and of course to drink, dance, and party. The festival even has its own beer pipeline to keep the beer flowing!

The National Team
Die Mannschaft

The European Championships and the World Cup are the few times that die-hard *Fußball* rivals get behind the one team that they can all cheer for: the German national team.

Which team has the **kickoff**?
*Welche Mannschaft hat **Anstoß**?*

That header was awesome!
Der Kopfstoß war echt der Hammer!

He's getting **the red card**!
*Der hat **die Arschkarte gezogen**!*

Since the ref pulls the red card out of his back pocket, it's called "drawing the ass card." The phrase can be used in soccer or to describe any situation where you're shit out of luck.

Was that a **bicycle kick**?
*War das 'n **Scherenschlag**?*

He's afraid of the **penalty kick**!
*Er hat Schiss vorm **Elfer**!*

Short for *elf meter schießen*, or the "11 meter shot."

So where are all the **hooligans**?
*Wo sind denn die ganzen **Hooligans**?*

Similar to hooligans the world over, German hooligans are mostly jerk-offs who hang around looking pissed and looking for a fight. The riot cops show up at train stations and stadiums on game days to help keep the peace, but seeing them decked out with their tactical shields and helmets can scare the shit out of newbies.

Dude, I really need get hooked up with the **club colors**!
*Alda, ich brauche doch 'ne coole **Kutte**!*

German soccer fans can kinda be like bikers. They drink a lot, get rowdy, and they wear their own colors. The *Kutte* is like a sleeveless jean jacket covered with about 50 patches from your favorite team on it. You'll probably find some dried blood or vomit on it, too.

Check out all the cute little **ball-boys**.
*Schau mal, die süßen **Auflaufkinder**.*

Also known as *Einlaufkinder*, these are the kids from the kiddy leagues who run out with the pro players on the field before matches. They're sort of like the team's mascots, but their only job is to stand there. The term literally means "kids that run out."

Aren't **scarves** kinda lame?

*Sind die **Schals** nicht etwas uncool?*

Like the *Kutte*, the team **scarf** is like a fan's version of a security blanket. They will bring it with them to every game, wear it even when it's not cold, and swing it at matches to get all fired up.

Opening procession

Einlauf (m)

This is the term for the procession of players, as they take to the field before the coin toss and kick-off. It's usually accompanied by lots of cheers, fireworks, fanfare, and the obligatory *Einlaufmusik*. Each team has their own song, or a favorite hit they've adopted.

I'd rather watch the game at the **Fan-zone**.

*Das Spiel würde ich lieber in der **Fan-zone** gucken.*

These are the massive outdoor viewing areas set up for the World Cup and European Championships. It's basically a giant tailgate party with better food and beer, plus you actually get to watch the match.

Cheering
Jubeln

German sports fans are totally fanatic—you might even say freakishly territorial—about their home teams. It all comes down to their hard-core regional identity as Berliners, Hamburgers, Bremers, Dresdners, etc. Rooting for anyone but the home team is the social equivalent of pissing in someone else's pool, and you're likely to get shunned at an early age for it.

Hurray!

Hurrah!

Gooooo!

Looooos!

Shoot!
Schieß los!

Goooooooal!
Tooooooor!

The **ref** is fuckin' nuts!
*Der **Schiri** hat 'ne Macke!*

Aw, come on!
Na, komm schon!

The goalie's got a **clubbed foot!**
*Der Schlussmann hat 'nen **Klumpfuß!***

Fuckin' Munich fans.
Scheiß München Fans.

Murder 'em!
Bringt sie um!

How can I get **season tickets**?
*Wie kriege ich eine **Dauerkarte**?*

Can you help me out with **the rules**?
*Kannste' mir mal die **Spielregeln** erklären?*

Are you a **hard-core fan**?
*Bist Du ein **hardcore Freak**?*

Are you FC St. Pauli **supporters**?
*Seid ihr FC St. Pauli **Retter**?*

Hamburg's FC St. Pauli is Germany's only punk-approved soccer club.
St. Pauli is famous for its punks, the *Reeperbahn*, and its red-light district.
In danger of going under due to lack of sponsors, *Retter*, or literally
"saviors," stepped in by buying tons of merch and drumming up interest
and sponsors for the club. Screw Bayern München; FC St. Pauli for life!

Do you know any cool **chants**?
*Kennste coole **Chants**?*

Exercise
Training

In general, Germans are pretty health conscious and try to stay active. Going to the gym and getting ridiculously pumped up like Arnie isn't as big as it is in the States, but most people join some sort of sports club or *Sportverein* where they really get into whichever sport twists their pretzel. Of course, it's not just exercise or training, but a way to hang out, and most importantly, even go out for a beer or two afterward. If you ask around, you're sure to find someone into the same activities as you are, and there's likely a club for it.

Hey, you guys know where I can...?
Hey, wisst ihr, wo ich...kann?

> **exercise**
> *trainieren*
>
> **do some sports**
> *Sport treiben*
>
> **box**
> *boxen*
>
> **find a gym**
> *ein Fitness Studio finden*
>
> **find a sporting club**
> *einen Sportverein finden*
>
> **lift some weights**
> *Gewichte heben*
>
> **go swimming**
> *schwimmen*

go jogging
joggen

do some circuit training
Circuittraining machen

go for a walk
spazieren gehen
Germany's favorite Sunday afternoon activity.

go for a hike
wander
Literally, "to wander," but Germans take their hiking very seriously. There are even *Wanderwege* or hiking trails that link various breweries together, and a special verb, *Bierwandern,* to describe the activity of hiking from one brewery to the next and drinking at each one. *Prost!*

I should do some more....
Ich sollte mehr....

warm-ups
aufwärmen

sit-ups
Aufrichter machen

push-ups
Liegestützen machen

pull-ups
Klimmzüge machen

squats
Kniebeugen machen

Should I work my...?
Sollte ich an meinen...arbeiten?

biceps
Bizeps

triceps
Trizeps

pecs
Brustmuskeln

thighs
Oberschenkeln

calves
Waden

glutes
Pomuskeln

gut
Bauchmuskeln

Should we go for a run?
Sollten wir laufen gehen?

I'm not a big fan of the **gym**!
*Ich bin kein großer Fan von **Muckibuden**!*
The *Muckibude* is literally the muscle shack.

I'm totally **sore**.
*Ich habe voll die **Muskelkater**.*

I'm **sweating like a pig**!
*Ich **schwitze wie Sau**!*

I'm totally **outta breath**!
*Ich bin voll **außer Atem**!*

I'm totally **worn out**!
*Ich bin voll **ausgepowert**!*
Literally, "out-powered."

I guess I could use **some practice**.
*Ich sollte vielleicht doch ein **bisschen üben**.*

CHAPTER 9

Food, Dining, & Cafés
Essen, Essen Gehend, & Cafés

Hunger
Hunger

When Germans get the munchies, they take ownership of
their growling guts by describing being hungry as "having
hunger" (*Hunger haben*). Letting everyone know how
hungry you are can be just as important as the food you eat
to quiet the monster in your belly, so express your need to
feed accordingly with the following morsels.

I'm....
Ich....

a little hungry
habe nur ein bisschen Hunger

hungry
habe Hunger

not hungry at all
habe keinen Hunger

famished
habe Schmacht

hungry as an animal!
habe tierischen Kohldampf!

starting to digest myself
verdaure mich gerade selbst

stuffed
bin satt

thirsty
habe Durst

parched
habe einen Brand

dying of thirst here
habe voll den Mordsbrand

I'm so hungry I could eat a horse.
Mein Magen hängt in den Kniekehlen.
Literally, "my stomach is hanging at my kneecaps."

My belly....
Mein Magen....

is empty
ist leer

is full
ist voll

is gonna burst
platzt gleich

is killing me
tut mir weh

is grumbling
knurrt

Food
Essen

Food is awesome. If you don't eat it, you die. Need I say more? Germans take eating pretty seriously. It's so important to them that they've got multiple words for it, be it *Lebensmittel* (the means of life), *Nahrungsmittel* (the means of nourishment), or simply *Essen* (food). Whether you're cooking at home, going out to grab a *Dönerkebab,* or just chilling and ordering a pizza, use these essentials to get by.

You eat yet?
Haste` schon gegessen?

Wanna **grab a bite**?
*Wollen wir was **ins Gesicht schieben**?*
Literally, "wanna shove something in your face?"

I gotta **eat something**.
*Ich muss **was essen**.*

Let's **pig out**!
*Lass uns **fressen**!*

What **do you like to eat**?
Was isst Du gern?

Is there a **health food store** around here?
*Gibt's irgendwo in der Nähe ein **Reformhaus/einen Bioladen**?*

Got anything... **vegetarian?/vegan/Gluten-free**?
*Gibt's was...**vegetarisches?/veganisches?/glutenfreies**?*

You can't get good **pretzels** anywhere in the U.S.
*In den Staaten kriegt man keine vernünftigen **Brezeln**.*

What's your **favorite food**?
*Was it dein **Lieblingsessen**?*

Should I **cook you up something**?
*Sollte ich dir **was kochen**?*

Let's **go out to eat**.
*Lass uns **essen gehen**.*

Maybe we should **call for takeout**.
*Vielleicht sollten wir **den Lieferservice anrufen**.*

You wanna just **order a pizza**?
*Willste' einfach **'ne Pizza bestellen**?*

I don't really like...food.
...Essen mag ich nicht so sehr.

Dude, **I'm jonesing** for something....
***Ich hab' voll Bock** auf was....*

I don't want something....
Ich hab null Bock auf was....

> **greasy**
> *fettiges*
>
> **healthy**
> *gesundes*
>
> **tasty**
> *leckeres*
>
> **exotic**
> *exotisches*
>
> **fancy**
> *feines*

vegetarian
vegetarisches

quick
schnelles

huge
großes

Eating out
Essen gehen

Most Germans like to cook at home rather than eat out. I had to convince a German roommate once that ordering a pizza didn't make me lazy, just hungry for pizza. When Germans go out to dinner, it's usually part of a night out, like before hitting the clubs or going out on a date. There aren't a lot of chain restaurants in Germany besides American fast food places, which are just as bad in Germany as they are in the States. But why waste your time on American fast food anyway? Every major German city has tons of great international restaurants to choose from, and Germans are always more than happy to recommend their favorite organic raw vegan Thai joint or whatever.

When deciding on a cuisine, instead of saying, "Let's go to an Italian restaurant," for example, make it casual by saying "*Lass uns zum Italiener*" ("Let's go to the Italians"), which is basically like saying "Let's grab some Italian" in English.

Let's grab some....
Lass uns zum....

Italian food

Italiener

If your idea of great Italian food is the Olive Garden, then you're in for a treat. Italian food in Germany is legit and is the closest to the real thing you'll find without getting run over by some dick on a Vespa in Rome.

Mexican food

Mexikaner

I'm from Southern California and love Mexican food. Mostly due to issues of proximity, Mexican food in Germany is almost nonexistent and when you can find it, it usually makes Taco Bell look gourmet. Of course, your new roommates will likely try to win you over with the "authentic" recipe they learned during their semester in Mexico, but don't be discouraged. Things are changing, and you can find some good tacos in Berlin or a tasty burrito in just about any larger city.

Indian food

Inder

Indian food is always great, but for some reason it's especially amazing in Germany. The menus are usually a weird mixture of English and German, which hilariously leads to descriptions like "hot dick curry," where the *dick* here just means it's thick.

Japanese food

Japaner

Is it just me, or are most Japanese restaurants in America owned by Korean or Chinese families? This seems to be the case for most sushi places in Germany, too. But, almost every major city will have a great place for you to get your raw fish fix.

Chinese food
Chinesen

Chinese food is not really all that different in Germany than it is in the States, except maybe less greasy. There are a lot of Chinese restaurants in the Fatherland, but they always seem empty and kinda sad.

Vietnamese food
Vietnamesen

East Germany had lots of guest workers from Vietnam who stayed after the Berlin Wall fell, and it seems like at least a third of them opened restaurants. A lot of them are a weird combination of Vietnamese and Chinese fast food, but there are some really good soup shops, too.

Turkish food
Türken

Turkish food is like the Mexican food of Germany. It's tasty, cheap, and available on nearly every corner. Turkish restaurants are especially prevalent in the north, and the Kreuzberg district in Berlin is the German birthplace of the delicious *Döner Kebab*.

Greek food
Griechen

Greek food rules. It's really similar to, and almost as popular as, Turkish food, but don't confuse the two or they might spit in your gyro.

Persian food
Perser

Lots of Persian restaurants will describe themselves as *Orientalisch* or "from the Orient." For those who failed their course on ancient civilization, it means Persia, not Asia. The food is insanely good and amazingly colorful and diverse. If you're a vegetarian, you're set, because there are tons of veggie dishes to choose from.

The snack shop
Imbiss

These small snack shops (*Imbiss* literally means "between the bite") are the German equivalents of taco trucks and roach coaches. They're also referred to as a *Pommesbude*, or French fry joints, even if they don't serve fries. They're the number one place where everyone from businessmen to punkers rub elbows and eat some really good street food on the cheap. Lots of legit restaurants also operate an *Imbiss* for people who want to eat on the run or while staggering home from a club. One of the most important things to remember is that *Imbiss*-slang (*Imbiss-deutsch*) is hard-core street slang...the closest thing you'll speak to scumbag German (*Asi-deutsch*) without actually being a scumbag. There are four golden rules:

1. Be brief when ordering. Hungry drunk people don't want to waste their time with extra words and syllables.

> **Fries with ketchup.**
> *Einmal Pommes mit Ketchup.*

2. Don't use articles. This is the one time you really don't need to use *der/die/das*, but if you do use an article, make sure it is *den*, the *Imbiss* article of choice regardless of gender or quantity.

The order of fries!
Den Pommes!

3. When you go to pick up your food, you don't say, "I ordered the sausage." You say, "I *am* the sausage."

I'm the sausage.
Ich bin den Wurst.

4. Never use plurals. If you want to order two or more of something, just use the number and the singular form of the noun.

Two bratwurst.
Zweimal Bratwurst.

Gimme a....
Einmal....

Döner (m)

Dönerkebab is the Turkish version of a gyro. It is prepared differently in every country where it is served, and in Germany, it caters to German tastes. Walk by almost any Turkish *Imbiss* and you'll see what looks like a giant cone of meat (usually lamb, beef, or sometimes chicken) spinning on a spit in an upright rotisserie. Stand mesmerized as the grill master slices off strips of the meat with a giant knife into an awaiting pita or *Fladenbrot* (Turkish flatbread) before it's garnished with pickled cabbage and a garlic-yogurt tzatziki sauce. Not into the meat? Order it vegetarian, *vegetarisch*, or without meat, *ohne Fleisch*. This is absolutely the best thing before, during, or after a night of hard partying.

As if the idea of bread stuffed with meat from a spit isn't attractive enough, some marketing genius in the *Döner* industry came up with this amazing slogan. It comes in handy when your friends ask why you are eating like five of them in a sitting.

Döner **makes you prettier!**
Döner macht schöner!

Pommes (pl)

German French fries make the average fries from a U.S. fast food joint taste like Mr. Potato Head's fried poop. *Pommes* are thick cut, double fried, and come with any kind of sauce imaginable. *Pommes rot/weiß* or *Pommes Schranke* gets you fries with mayonnaise and ketchup.

Frikadelle (f)

Sometimes called *Bulette, Klopse, Frika,* or *Grilletta,* this is the granddaddy of the American hamburger. *Frikadellen* look a little like football-shaped hamburgers. The meat's got garlic, onion, and a few other spices in it, and is far superior to just about anything you call a burger. Eat one in the morning with a roll and mustard, and you'll forget that you were ever hungover.

Lahmacun (f)

Turkish pizza isn't really pizza, but thin Turkish bread with spices and sauce. But it's close enough. Try one rolled up with *Dönerkebab* meat in it.

Brötchen (n)

These little rolls are a German staple. No matter how hungover your friends are, at least one will crawl down to the baker and buy a bag of these so everyone can eat breakfast. Butter them up, throw on some jam or cheese and meat, and you're golden.

Schnitzel (n)

Thin, breaded, fried meat, usually veal or pork, but can also be chicken, turkey, or even tofu for you animal-friendly types. Squeeze a lemon over it and wolf it down with a plate of fries and a nice cold beer...or just ask for a

Schnipopi, short for *Schnitzel, Pommes, und Pils* (Schnitzel, fries, and a beer).

Because Germans don't dick around when it comes to sausage, here's the best of the *Wurst*:

Currywurst (f)

Also referred to as just a *C-wurst*. The Hamburg-Berlin rivalry is brutal when it comes to who makes the best of these sliced-up sausages doused in ketchup and curry powder. A *C-wurst* is the next best thing to *Döner* for your drunken crawls home. If you're ever in the St. Pauli district in Hamburg, be sure to hit up the *Imbiss bei Schorsch* for one of these. They're the king of the *C-wurst*.

Bockwurst (f)

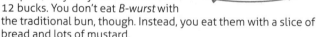

Also called *B-wurst*, these are like those foot-long dogs from the ballpark, only they don't suck or cost 12 bucks. You don't eat *B-wurst* with the traditional bun, though. Instead, you eat them with a slice of bread and lots of mustard.

Presskopf (m)

Did you know that head cheese is really a kind of sausage? It's really kind of gross, too.

Zungenwurst (f)

Like head cheese, but made from cows' tongues instead of the meat around the head.

Blutwurst (f)

Blood sausage is, well, sausage made from cooked blood, grains, and some pig fat. It tastes like a deliciously rusty nail.

Knackwurst (f)

Named after the cracking sound they make when you bite into the natural intestinal casing. Their contents vary from region to region.

Leberwurst (f)

This is straight up liver sausage, but don't think of calling it liverwurst. It's a fantastic concoction of liver, spices, pork, and other innards.

Teewurst (f)

No one really knows why it's called "tea sausage" but with 40 percent fat, it's basically meat butter.

Wattwurm (f)

From *Ostfriesland* in the northwest, these "mud worms" are like smokier, saltier, foot-and-a-half-long Slim Jims. They're great with beer. Think of them as meat pretzels.

Bratwurst (f)

Any grilled sausage. Usually, but not always, pork or beef. See below.

Rossbratwurst (f)

Horse: the other *Bratwürste* meat. I'm not sure how you feel about eating Mr. Ed, but these are rare and immensely tasty treats. Get them at the *Freimarkt* in Bremen.

Thüringer Bratwurst(f)

Made with garlic and spices, these flavorful favorites from the southeast are the king of the *Bratwürste*.

Nürnberger Bratwurst (f)

In German, the saying "*Aller guten Dinge sind drei*" means "good things come in threes" and is the equivalent of "third time's a charm!" That's definitely the case with these little sausages. Get them in groups of three from your favorite *Imbiss*, and try not to go back for two more rounds...I dare you.

Weißwurst (f)

Despite what you might think a "white sausage" is, these Bavarian beauties are made from a weird mixture of pork, veal, and ice. No joke, ice. You'll probably eat and throw up like 40 of these at Oktoberfest.

Tofuwurst (f)
Even though I'm no longer a vegetarian, I do appreciate the fact that the health conscious Germans make a pretty mean veggie version of just about every type of meat sausage.

Weird German specialties

Any of your lessons on German cuisine were sure to include examples of recipes that seem pretty tame and align with general Western food tastes. Although it's true that Germans don't eat many weird animals or insects, like some cultures in the rest of the world, they do have some insane dishes made from ingredients and animal parts that you might likely throw out. If you really want to get the most out of your culinary experiences, I encourage you to try any of these delicacies.

NORTHERN GERMANY
DER NORDEN
Bremer Kükenragout (m)
This "baby chicken stew" is a rare delicacy that both intrigues and disgusts at the same time. It's made with young chickens, shrimp, crawfish tails, and beef tongue. Yumm!

Grünkohl und Pinkel (m)
Northern German soul food. *Grünkohl* is steamed kale cooked with super salty bacon that you eat with a special sausage called *Pinkel*. *Pinkel* actually gets its name from the verb to piss, or *pinkeln*, since when these sausages get cooked, they drip from the tip as if pissing. In the northwest, where this originates, groups organize a *Kohlfahrt*, or "Kohl-trip" where everyone piles into a bus, gets incredibly drunk, and pigs out on this dish.

Schwarzsauer (m)

This blood soup originated in eastern Prussia, but still delights and terrifies northern Germans to this day. It's essentially pig's blood, vinegar, some leftover meat scraps, and pork fat. The vinegar turns the blood black (*Schwarz*) and is sour (*sauer*), hence the incredibly creative name.

Eisbein (n)

A Berlin tradition, *Eisbein* is boiled "pig knuckle" or pork hock (everywhere else in Germany, it's called *Schweinshaxe*); and it is roasted so it stays juicy and you can pull it off the bone. It's served on a

bed of *Sauerkraut*, mashed potatoes, and peas, and with tons of beer. It looks gruesome, but is a pork lover's dream.

Moppelkotze (f)

What can you say about a stew that is lovingly referred to as "puppy puke"? Not much, other than that's how some northern Germans refer to an *Eintopf*, or "one-pot." There's no set recipe to an *Eintopf*; you just throw whatever stew-friendly ingredients you have around into a pot and let it stew. I guess the end result does look kinda pukey.

CENTRAL GERMANY
MITTELDEUTSCHLAND
Saumagen (m)

Another creatively titled dish. Sow's stomach is pretty much the German version of a Scottish haggis, only all the ingredients (vegetables, pork, spices, and potatoes) are stuffed into a pig's stomach and cooked. You eat the stuffing and leave the stomach.

Handkäse mit Musik (m)

Traditional pub-grub from the central German state of Hessen. This "hand-cheese with music" is a kind of waxy cheese that's served with an herb dressing and sliced onions. The name comes from the fact that if you eat a lot of cheese and onions, you're probably gonna make ass music all night. Most *Kneipen* owners offer a version "without music," too, as a courtesy to the other guests. But if you're gonna try it just once, you might as well go for the real deal. Remember to wash it down with lots of hard German cider and you'll fit right in.

Sauerbraten (m)

This "sour roast" is traditionally made from horse meat, though today it's more often beef, marinated in a vinegar spice mixture before roasting. Eat it with *Rotkohl*, the delicious pickled red cabbage cousin to *Sauerkraut*.

SOUTHERN GERMANY
SÜDDEUTSCHLAND
Hasenpfeffer (m)

A Black Forest specialty consisting of all the gruesome, leftover parts of a rabbit cooked in a peppery stew. You can also get the same thing with pork (*Schweinepfeffer*) or goose (*Gänsepfeffer*) if eating Bugs Bunny bums you out.

Flädlesuppe (f)

This is basically pancake soup, and yes, it's as weird as it sounds. If you end up in *Baden Württemberg*, make sure you at least get a look at this. It's beef broth served with coils of crepe-like pancakes in it.

Leberkäse (m)

A sort of sausage loaf that looks like a square of bologna and comes served with either an egg (sunny-side up) and mashed potatoes, or warm with a roll and mustard. The markets in Munich sell this stuff like crazy. Try it if you're starving or like eating giant meat-flavored erasers.

Fast food
Fastfood

Germans have a love-hate relationship with fast food. The socially conscious part of them despises the idea of chains and the lack of nutritional value, but the lazy, antisocial, hungover side of them craves the McDrive. If they do eat at a fast food joint, they do so begrudgingly, making fun of it at the same time. And their regional pride usually kicks in, too, making them more inclined to choose a locally owned fast food joint rather than a larger international chain. These German fast food outlets are supposedly healthier than their international (i.e., U.S.) counterparts, something the health-conscious Krauts dig. That being said, you can still get your grease on at any of the following.

Do you really want to eat at...?
Willste' wirklich bei....essen?

I can't eat at...anymore.
Ich kann nie wieder bei...essen.

...is worse than eating out of a trash can.
...ist schlimmer als aus der Mülltonne zu essen.

> ### Nordsee
> Where else can you get a cold fish sandwich (*Fischbrötchen*)? Okay, in Germany, you can get those almost anywhere, but *Nordsee* shreds, and I don't even like fish.
>
> ### Wienerwald
> This is a fast food chicken joint from Austria whose name means "the Viennese forest." Sure, it sounds pretty magical, but it's really just a Euro version of KFC. At least

the chicken here is roasted instead of fried and doesn't taste like a greasy sponge.

Kochlöffel

The "Cooking Spoon" is a truly German fast food chain that's been around since the '60s. They do chicken and burgers and are the only place I know of in Germany where you can get those weird fried meat croquets you find in Dutch vending machines. Those things look like fried cat turds but taste delicious, even when you're sober.

McDonald's

Germans call it *McDoof* (McStupid), but on occasion they'll still eat here, 'cause if they didn't, the golden arches would have gone out of business years ago. The drive-thru is called McDrive and every one of them serves beer.

Burger King

Lovingly referred to as *Würger Schling* (the hangman's noose).

Kentucky Fried Chicken

Everyone in Germany calls KFC "Kentucky *schreit ficken*" because it rhymes with "Kentucky Fried Chicken" but means "Kentucky scream fuck." Apparently, this is funny to Germans. In addition to mediocre fried chicken, KFC serves donuts and chili cheese fries, too.

Pizza Hut

Their slogan is "The American Way of Pizza." It's about as "good" as it is in the States, but the one near my house had an all-you-can-eat-pizza night with free soda refills. Since no German restaurants—fast food or otherwise—offer free refills, this is like finding money in the street.

Cafés
Cafés

Though it may seem like there's a Starbucks on every corner, American-style coffee chains are kinda new in Germany, and the serious coffee-drinking Germans have taken a while to warm up to them. The Germans are an enviro-conscious bunch and cringe a bit at the thought of all those paper cups, plastic lids, and the "coffee to go" culture that flies in the face of their idea of coffee as a leisure activity. Nevertheless, "American-style" coffee houses have popped up. But unsurprisingly, in mega-corporation-hating Germany, smaller chains tend to do far better than that global coffee monolith from Seattle. In fact, the corporate coffee concept is so foreign to Germans that Starbucks had to come up with a worksheet to help customers order using their annoying brand of barrista-speak.

Tchibo
They pioneered the term "coffee to go" and have got coffee shops, a travel agency, and a mail-order catalog all in one shop. If you got a crappy gift from some German aunt, it probably came from Tchibo.

Balzac Coffee
It's pretty much the German version of Starbucks. You can even get bubble tea here, with those weird tapioca balls.

Woytons
This is a smaller chain that serves your usual café assortment of soup, salads, sandwiches, and snacks. The fact that they're a smaller chain makes them cool, but it also helps that they don't play outdated alternative rock on the sound system.

Bagel Brothers

This is really the only place to go for bagels because, well, it's really the only place in Germany that makes bagels. That's not a bad thing, though, 'cause the bagels here are pretty kick-ass.

Ditsch

Not really a coffee shop, but I wanted to give them some cred because of the wonders they work with pretzels. Seriously, it's scary how good these things are. If you're a fan of pizza bagels, you'll freak out over the *Tomaten-Käse Stange*: a pretzel-pizza roll that tastes like nothing you've ever had before. I ate six of these in one sitting once and felt like a pretzel god.

LeCrobag

Peddlers of coffee and "French-style" pastries, which consist mostly of croissants filled with anything imaginable. The marzipan ones are the best, even if you're not a 12-year-old kid. Like *Ditsch*, you'll find a *LeCrobag* at nearly every subway or train station.

Yummmmy!
Lecker!

Another cultural tidbit that was likely left out of your textbook is that medieval Germans used to burp and fart at the table as a sign of satisfaction and gratitude. Luckily, the Germans have emerged from the Dark Ages and you no longer have to thank your host by airing out your large intestine. These days, if you really want to show that you're enjoying yourself, let everyone know with some of these phrases.

Delectable!
Schmackofatzig!

Hmmm, **tasty tasty!**
*Hmmm, **legga legga**!*

That was **amazing**.
*Das war aber **herrlich**.*

You're totally **mowing that down**.
*Das haste' voll **aufgezehrt**.*

Wow, you can really **shovel it in**!
*Mannomann, kannst Du was **wegschaufeln**!*

Awesome, totally **awesome**.
*Fabelhaft, einfach **fabelhaft**.*

The cook's **a total genius**.
*Der Koch ist **ein Genie**.*

Oh boy, **this is the shit!**
*Heidewitzka, **ist das aber legga**!*

Can I get **seconds**?
*Gibt's 'nen **Nachschlag**?*

That smells **incredible**.
*Das riecht aber **wunderbar**.*

Yuck!
Bäähh!

You know that bald guy on TV who travels the world eating bull balls and pig brains? On German TV, he's called *Der Alles-Esser*, or "the guy who eats everything." He eats tons of nasty "cuisine," but never gets grossed out. Impress your friends by showing your disgust the next time you see him chowing down on monkey rectum.

Disgusting!
Widerlich!

That's totally **icky**.
*Das ist aber voll **ekelig**.*

That's gross!
Pfui!

That's really gross!
Pfui extra!

That's really fucking gross!
Pfui extra gold!

This looks like a **shitheap**.
*Das sieht aus wie ein **Misthaufen**.*

I don't like how...tastes.
...schmeckt mir nicht.

...tastes **nasty**.
*...schmeckt aber **ekelhaft**.*

...tastes **like shit**.
*...schmeckt **wie Scheiße**.*

...smells like **baby poo**.
*...riecht **wie Baby A-A**.*
pronounced like "ah-ah"

...smells like **the morgue**.
*...stink **wie die Leichenhalle**.*

> **Sauerkraut**
> *Sauerkraut (n)*
>
> **Cauliflower**
> *Blumenkohl (m)*
>
> **Liverwurst**
> *Leberwurst (f)*

Swiss cheese
Emmentaler (m)

What's that **smell**?
*Was ist das für ein **Gestank**?*

That shit **reeks**.
*Das **riecht aber übel**.*

No thanks, **I don't eat poop**.
*Nee, **Kacke esse ich nicht**.*

I can't eat this.
Sowas kann ich nicht essen.

You really **gonna eat that shit**?
*Willst Du **den Scheiß wirklich essen**?*

This place is really **crappy**.
*Die Bude hier ist **das Allerletzte**.*

Call an ambulance, **I'm gonna be sick**!
*Ruf den Notarzt, **mir wird's schlecht**!*

Let's **bail**.
*Lass uns **abhauen**.*

....

Check please!
Die Rechnung bitte!

The food at most *Kneipen, Gaststätten,* and *Lokale* is usually
pretty good, but being accustomed to the overly friendly
service culture in the USA, the wait staff will likely seem
crappy. It's not unusual to find yourself waiting around for
your bill while your waiter disappears for a smoke or even
a beer. What you perceive as lousy service is the result of
a culture that prefers to leave diners alone to enjoy their

meal, rather than bug them. It doesn't help that tax and tip are technically included in the cost of your meal, giving waiters little incentive to go the extra mile. Additional tipping is becoming much more expected these days, however. Though it's not yet on par with the 15–20 percent you're expected to leave in the States, it's now customary to leave 10 percent.

Pardon me...?
Entschuldigung...?

> can I see **the menu**
> *darf ich **die Karte** sehen*

> got any **specials**
> *gibt's ein **Tagesmenü***

> what do you **recommend**
> *was **empfehlen** Sie*

> is there **meat in that**
> *gibt's **Fleisch drin***

Is that organic?
*Ist das **Bio**?*

How big are the portions?
*Wie groß sind **die Portionen**?*

We'd like to order.
*Wir möchten gerne **bestellen**.*

Can I get a knife?
*Darf ich auch **ein Messer** haben?*

Can I get that without...?
*Kriege ich das auch **ohne**...?*

> **tomatoes**
> *Tomaten (pl)*

mushrooms
Champignons (pl)

bacon
Speck (m)

cheese
Käse (m)

I didn't order **this crap**.
Diesen Dreck habe ich nicht bestellt.

Do you have **dessert** too?
Gibt's auch Nachtisch?

This **looks a little weird**.
Das hier sieht komisch aus.

We're **in kind of a hurry**.
Wir habn's aber etwas eilig.

We wanna **pay**.
Wir wollen zahlen.

Can you **wrap that up to go**?
Können Sie das einpacken?

When's your **shift end**?
Wann haste` Feierabend?

Acknowledgments

Für ihre Hilfe und Inspiration möchte ich mich bei Drs. Jeffrey L. High, Carrie Collenberg-Gonzalez, Nicholas Martin, Jutta Birmele, Walo Deuber und Wilm Pelters ganz herzlich bedanken. Ohne sie, wäre ich nie Germanist geworden. Ein warmes Dankeschön an die vielen Freunde, die mir ihren Rat, ihre Zeit, Hilfe und vor allem ihre Freundschaft geschenkt haben; H.H.H und Sabine Preuß, Stefan Harbers, Timm und Heike Sander, Lothar Grüning, Matthias „Perry" Fecht, Jens-Olaf Pampus, Matthias Kopf, Andrea Jablonski, Harald Friedl und Barbara Neuwirth, Erich von Kneip und Maren Wood, Christoph Döhne, und Sandra Kretschmer und SK und SM. Einen besonderen Dank möchte ich an die Familie Krampe richten. Für ihre endlosen Hugz + Luvz, für ihr Verständnis und Vertrauen und vor allem für ihre Liebe danke ich den wichtigsten Deutschen meines Lebens; Francesca Krampe und Damon Baird.

Tremendous thanks to the Chavez family for accepting so many of my friends from faraway places into their home. Thanks to all the Chaffeys, for helping me in more ways than they will ever know. Thanks to Jello, Tim, and my brother Kevin for encouraging and contributing to my twisted sense of humor. To my parents for their love, support, and for allowing me the freedom to choose my own path, I am eternally grateful.

About the Author

Daniel Chaffey is a writer, scholar, educator, and eternal student of all things German. He has lived and worked in Germany as a student, Fulbright teaching associate, translator, and bartender, where he perfected his high German skills and also learned to converse like a German sailor. He holds an MA in German Studies and a teaching credential from Cal State Long Beach, where he was also a lecturer in German Studies.